All at Sea

Memories of Maritime Merseyside

Compiled by
Ev Draper

Foreword by
Linda McDermott - BBC Radio Merseyside

Introduction by
David Roberts - Maritime Historian

95.8 FM BBC RADIO MERSEYSIDE

95.8 FM **B B C** RADIO MERSEYSIDE

in association with

Avid Publications
Garth Boulevard
Bebington, Wirral,
Merseyside.
CH63 5LS

Telephone / Fax: (44) 0151 645 2047
e-mail info @ AvidPublications.co.uk
website http//www.AvidPublications

All At Sea
- Memories of Maritime Merseyside
Compiled by
Ev Draper

084251739

ISBN 1 902964 12 8

Editing, Typeset and cover design by William David Roberts © 2000
Avid Publications.

Cover: The "Antenor" and tugs, in the Mersey.
Reproduction by permission of marine artist Les Cowle

CANADIAN   PACIFIC

WELCOME

TO THE

Empress of France

The Captain and Officers welcome you and hope you will enjoy your voyage with them.

The Chief Steward and his Staff are always at your service — — do not hesitate to call upon them at any time.

Your accommodation is Berth...........Deck...........Room..........

Please have this card readily available for presentation at gangway.

Canadian Pacific Welcome Card

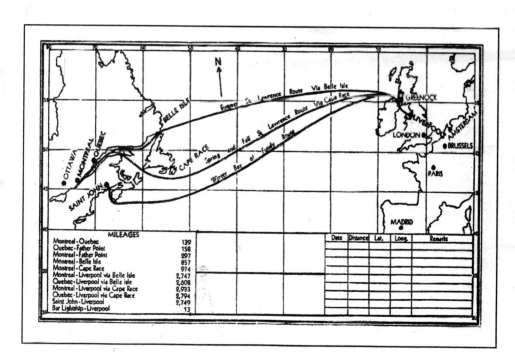

CPR Route Map

WHITE EMPRESS SAILINGS

Leave Montreal	Leave St. John	Arrive Greenock	Arrive Liverpool	Steamship	Leave Liverpool	Leave Greenock	Arrive Quebec	Arrive Montreal	Arrive St. John
1954	1954	1954	1954		1954	1954	1954	1954	1954
—	Jan. 26	—	Feb. 3	Empress of Australia	—	—	—	—	—
—	—	—	—	Empress of France	Feb. 3	—	—	—	Feb. 10
—	Feb. 17	—	Feb. 24	Empress of France	Mar. 3	—	—	—	Mar. 10
—	—	—	—	Empress of Australia	Mar. 10	—	—	—	Mar. 18
—	Mar. 17	—	Mar. 24	Empress of France	Mar. 30	—	—	—	Apr. 6
—	Mar. 24	—	Apr. 1	Empress of Australia	This westbound sailing to Montreal				
Leave New York Mar. 29 direct to Liverpool				Empress of Scotland	This westbound sailing to Montreal				
—	Apr. 9	—	Apr. 16	Empress of France	This westbound sailing to Montreal				
—	—	—	—	Empress of Australia	Apr. 9	—	Apr. 17	Apr. 17	—
—	—	—	—	Empress of Scotland	Apr. 16	Apr. 17	Apr. 23	Apr. 23	—
—	—	—	—	Empress of France	Apr. 23	—	Apr. 30	Apr. 30	—
Apr. 19	—	—	Apr. 27	Empress of Australia	Apr. 30	—	May 8	May 8	—
Apr. 27	—	May 3	May 4	Empress of Scotland	May 7	May 8	May 14	May 14	—
May 4	—	—	May 11	Empress of France	May 14	—	May 21	May 21	—
May 10	—	—	May 18	Empress of Australia	May 21	—	May 29	May 29	—
May 18	—	May 24	May 25	Empress of Scotland	May 28	May 29	June 4	June 4	—
May 25	—	—	June 1	Empress of France	June 4	—	June 10	June 11	—
May 31	—	—	June 8	Empress of Australia	June 11	—	June 18	June 19	—
June 8	—	June 14	June 15	Empress of Scotland	June 18	June 19	June 24	June 25	—
June 15	—	—	June 22	Empress of France	June 25	—	July 1	July 2	—
June 21	—	—	June 29	Empress of Australia	July 2	—	July 9	July 10	—
June 29	—	July 5	July 6	Empress of Scotland	July 9	July 10	July 15	July 16	—
July 6	—	—	July 13	Empress of France	July 16	—	July 22	July 23	—
July 12	—	—	July 20	Empress of Australia	July 23	—	July 30	July 31	—
July 20	—	July 26	July 27	Empress of Scotland	July 30	July 31	Aug. 5	Aug. 6	—
July 27	—	—	Aug. 3	Empress of France	Aug. 6	—	Aug. 12	Aug. 13	—
Aug. 2	—	—	Aug. 10	Empress of Australia	Aug. 13	—	Aug. 20	Aug. 21	—
Aug. 10	—	Aug. 16	Aug. 17	Empress of Scotland	Aug. 20	Aug. 21	Aug. 26	Aug. 27	—
Aug. 17	—	—	Aug. 24	Empress of France	Aug. 27	—	Sept. 2	Sept. 3	—
Aug. 23	—	—	Aug. 31	Empress of Australia	Sept. 3	—	Sept. 10	Sept. 11	—
Aug. 31	—	Sept. 6	Sept. 7	Empress of Scotland	Sept. 10	Sept. 11	Sept. 16	Sept. 17	—
Sept. 7	—	—	Sept. 14	Empress of France	Sept. 17	—	Sept. 23	Sept. 24	—
Sept. 13	—	—	Sept. 21	Empress of Australia	Sept. 24	—	Oct. 1	Oct. 2	—
*Sept. 21	—	Sept. 27	Sept. 28	Empress of Scotland	Oct. 1	Oct. 2	Oct. 7	Oct. 8	—
Sept. 28	—	—	Oct. 5	Empress of France	Oct. 8	—	Oct. 14	Oct. 15	—
Oct. 4	—	—	Oct. 12	Empress of Australia	Oct. 15	—	Oct. 22	Oct. 23	—
*Oct. 12	—	Oct. 18	Oct. 19	Empress of Scotland	Oct. 22	Oct. 23	Oct. 28	Oct. 29	—
Oct. 19	—	—	Oct. 26	Empress of France	Oct. 29	—	Nov. 4	Nov. 5	—
Oct. 25	—	—	Nov. 2	Empress of Australia	Nov. 5	—	Nov. 12	Nov. 13	—
*Nov. 2	—	Nov. 8	Nov. 9	Empress of Scotland	Cruising - Winter Months				

*Sails at daybreak. Passengers embark evening previous, commencing 8.00 p.m. Eastern Standard Time.

White Empress Sailings 1954 - Liverpool to Canada

10

CONTENTS

Foreword by Linda McDermott   v

Acknowledgements   vi

Introduction by David Roberts   vii

Chapter One - **Man and Boy**   1

Chapter Two -   **For those in Peril**   17

Chapter Three - **All Ashore**   43

Chapter Four - **Guiding Lights**   59

Chapter Five - **Trade Winds**   73

Chapter Six - **Women and the Sea**   87

Chapter Seven - **The 'Pool**   101

FOREWORD
by
Linda McDermott : BBC Radio Merseyside

I was born within an anchor-chains length of the sea. As a little girl, the Mersey was part of the fabric of my life.

I lived in Scotland Road, an area that provided the Merchant Navy with more men than any other part of Britain. Many of the men in my family went away to sea, and I remember how enthralled I would be listening to their tales of adventures in exotic sounding lands.

As a small child, I marvelled at the presents they brought back - a talking doll from New York, beads from Sierra Leone. I remember Uncle Jimmy making his way up the hill from the dock road with Persian rugs over his shoulder, for my grandmother, and Uncle John carefully carrying back the latest of a collection of china tea-sets for Gran from some far off country to which he sailed. I polish them with pride to this day.

With such beginnings it's no surprise that it instilled in me a passion for the sea, and a deep admiration for the men of Merseyside who went to see what was beyond the horizon. Their courage under fire during both world wars never ceases to amaze and move me.

It was a joy for me to compile the *All at Sea* programmes for BBC Radio Merseyside, programmes which celebrated our maritime history, and which in no small part inspired this collection of wonderful memories.

I have greatly enjoyed reading this book by Ev Draper. I know it will be of huge interest to all those who love ships and the sea, and who are proud of our incredible maritime history.

Acknowledgements

Thanks to all the contributors to this book, for their memories, and their memorabilia.

Thanks also go to the Liverpool Daily Post and Echo, "Reflections, c/o www.20thcenturyimages.com", marine artist Les Cowle, and the Archive Section of Liverpool Central Library, for their courtesy in allowing reproduction of various images.

And finally, a big "thank you" to local poet Jimmy McAleer, for his contributions to this volume.

INTRODUCTION

They say that we have all been touched at some time by the sea. For myself I come from a sea going and shipbuilding background. After serving in the Royal Navy during the Second World War my father spent most of his working life as a Cammell Laird shipbuilder, and I grew up with his stories of runs ashore at Trincomalee and Bombay. I too started my adult life by serving an apprenticeship at Lairds...looking back, some of the happiest days of my life.

The sea seems to touch something special in the British psyche, perhaps because we are an island race that imports much of our food and we also know that these islands have, in the past, had to be fought for. To the people of Merseyside this 'special relationship' with the sea seems a particularly strong bond...and this is never more true when you read some of the stories in this book.

As someone who has been contributing to Radio Merseyside for many years telling stories about ships and the sea I was highly enthusiastic about being involved with *All at Sea*, this latest addition to our maritime history compiled by Ev Draper.

Ev has worked hard to record these oral histories to preserve our regions reputation and its service to our country. Yet even Ev has sometimes been surprised by what she has found. Talking to her about the project she mentioned that some of those that she had talked to 'had cried' on retelling their tale of war or peace. It is a testimony to those who cried of the enormity of what they endured for the rest of us to survive, and I thank them all for their tears.

The importance of Merseyside's maritime heritage cannot be overstated. Make no mistake, our port and our river will live forever in the annals of Britain's history. Times change, but the River Mersey never changes as it ebbs and flows down the centuries, it will always be there for us and for our children so it is right and fitting that we should record the voices of those who worked on and around it during their lifetimes.

These are the voices of the men and women who sailed from the Mersey and took its name throughout the seven seas; who maintained the ships and kept them safe; who for trade or defence took our unique Scouse accent everywhere from Philadelphia to Penang.

We should all be very proud of them. I know I am.

David Roberts MA - Maritime Historian

Chapter One: Man and Boy

'I'll sail the stormy China Sea
Where Poseidon sleeps I'll go,
I'll see Valparaiso, Montevideo and Java,
Down where the trade winds blow.'

The days when boys ran away to sea are long gone; so is the often punitive training. But the memories that follow are full of humour, of companionship, and of someone always looking out for you.

Rodney Watch, the *"Conway"*

Puddin' and pie fellows

I was born in 1899, and I was about eleven or twelve when I was on the training ship, the "*Indefatigable*", she was an old capture from Trafalgar. Mother had to apply for a place for me, and you went before a committee. "Has the boy been before a magistrate?" Well, I had, but they never found out!

She was moored off New Ferry, in the river. The "*Conway*", now, you had to pay £300 a year for that, and we used to call them the "puddin' and pie" fellows. Some lads on the "*Indefatigable*", seaman's orphans, were as young as eight or nine. There were three hundred lads, rough and ready, always hungry.

You'd see schooners then, they waited off Rock Ferry, New Ferry, and as soon as the wind went southerly, you'd see them all sailing Down the river, forty or fifty of them, how they didn't collide, I don't know. I did two years and nine months.

Then I joined the "*Warrior*", a Harrison Line boat, to South Africa. 1/- a day, deck boy.

On the way out, a fireman died, they put him over the side and two of us, only lads, they got us to go down the stoke hole. We'd been working coal, about two hundred tons from one of the decks down to the hole. After two or three weeks of it, I said I'd had enough and went and told the Chief engineer to keep his job. I used to come down that stoke hole full of black dust, right into my bunk, too tired to wash or eat.

At the end of the trip, three months and twenty two days, we docked in London. I had £3 in gold, half a sovereign in gold and when I got to Lime

The *"Indefatigable"*- Courtesy Liverpool Daily Post and Echo

Salthouse Dock, 1932. Courtesy Liverpool Daily Post and Echo

Street, I walked home to Litherland, and put the money right into my mother's hand.

William Tennant - Bootle

A Home from Home?

My mother died when I was five, and I was sent to various Waifs and Strays homes. At that time, they were sending orphans out to Canada and Australia, and telling them they would get land when they were twenty one. I didn't want that, so I followed my brother to the "*Indefatigable*", on the Mersey. She was moved to Wales because of the blitz. When I first went there I was still school age, about thirteen and a half I'd be. We had schooling in the morning, and then seamanship, knots, morse code, boxing the compass, all things like that in the afternoon.

They had various initiations, when you were one month aboard, all those who'd been there longer than you gave you a punch on your arm, but eventually they stopped that.

You got the rope's end if you did anything bad. I didn't smoke at the time, went ashore, and took ten "Players" back for one of the lads. You lined up when you got back on board and the officer of the watch said "Off caps", and all the ciggies fell out. So I got six of the rope's end on my bare backside, and they kept it in a bucket of brine, so you can imagine how painful it was.

Every Friday you had what they called "dickie muster", you all stripped off, you went before the doctor, and you had a big basin of warm Epsom salts that you had to drink, and then they examined you all over. No dignity whatsoever.

Arthur Burch - Woolton

3

Trawlers in the Mersey

I can remember when I was a kid of seven or eight, we used to run around the docks. We were always hungry, and if a ship came in with fruit, like Youds, or Bibby's (they had nuts), we'd go aboard and scrounge a meal and the cook would have us cleaning the pans.

A few years later, when I was just on thirteen, things were tough, so I ran away to sea. I started off on the trawlers, the first was the "*Eileen Duncan*". I was the deck boy.

You never got your clothes off for about 12 days, you had a straw mattress and a blanket, and when you got out past the Isle of Man, you'd drop your nets and you'd drift, fishing for cod, hake, everything.

I had to throw ice on the fish, on board. You'd have to mend the nets, too. We berthed in Salthouse Dock, and you'd have to work all night to get the fish up to St. John's market.

I got a shilling a day.

Mick Sheehan - Canada

Singing for your Supper

It was called the Outward Bound Sea School in Aberdovey...the most worrying part was we spent four days on the sailing ship called the "*Warspite*", and when it was your turn to join her, you rowed out with your watch in a craft called a whaler.

And off we'd go into the Irish Sea. We had to take a small piece of rope, up the rigging, and feed the rope through a block and bring it down again. One young man froze up on the rigging, and I can recall Stan Hugill saying "No, leave him, you've done it, he'll do it". In the end, though, he was brought down.

Stan was probably one of the last men who sailed the oceans of the world under sail. He was the Shanty Man there and many of the duties we carried out were the same as in the days of Lord Nelson, pulling in the anchor, hoisting the rigging, it was all done to the shanties.

Stan taught us what were called shanty notes, almost like banshee wails which were part of the art of singing shanties. I remember being delegated to row ashore, collect sand from the beach, (which is now illegal), and then, with our bottoms facing sternwards, three abreast on either side of the deck, and with our sand, our house brick and a bucket of salt water we all moved in a motion together, scrubbing forward and backward, and this brought up the deck back to its original nice white condition. This was done every time we anchored.

We sang while we did it, one I can remember is "Whiskey is the Life of Man, Whiskey Johnny".

Colin Sharp -Bromborough

Kippers and Wales

Blue Funnel came to my school to ask for people who wanted to go to sea, and I'd lost my brother at sea, so I went to Aberdovey.

They used to have a hike, as they called it, they gave you a packet of kipper sandwiches, a torch, a map and a compass, and you had to find your way back to the school, over Cader Idris, 35 miles.

Stan Amos - Moreton

Knowing your place

It would be 1950, I was at the *"Conway"* - we were like stewards there, serving the cadets, looking after the ward rooms.

They used to call me the country boy, because I'd come from a small village in Sussex.

I did my first voyage on a ship called the *"Jason"*, out to Australia, and I remember the stewards didn't talk to the stewards' boys.

Bryan Wickens - Upton

Reaching New Heights

I volunteered in 1942 - for five years. I did not want to go into army, and do square bashing.

I did my training in HMS *"Ganges"*, Ipswich. They used to have a big mast there, three hundred ft. high, and you had to climb that, and the lads were crying at the bottom, they didn't want to go up. They said if you did not go up, your pay book will be stamped "Coward", and that would follow you. You had to go to the baths, as well, and they were all crying "I can't swim, can't swim", so they just threw them in.

It was freezing cold in 1942, we just had a singlet and a pair of pumps.

Punishment was fourteen days jankers, with a full kit on your back. It made you hard.

Tommy Clark - Runcorn

HMS "*Conway*" Courtesy Liverpool Daily Post and Echo

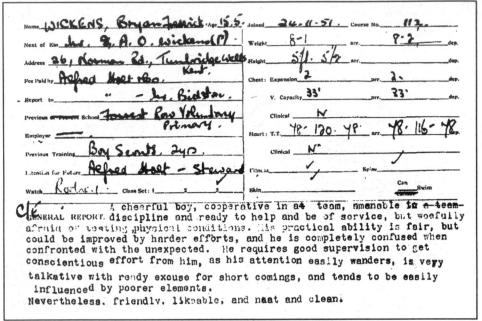

Name	WICKENS, Bryan Patrick Age 15.5	Joined 24.11.51	Course No. 112		

The report card (handwritten form):

Name WICKENS, Bryan Patrick. Age 15.5 Joined 24.11.51 Course No. 112
Next of Kin Mr. & A. O. Wickens (F)   Weight 8-1 arr. 9.2 dep.
Address 36, Norman Rd., Tunbridge Wells Kent.   Height 5ft. 5½ arr. ___ dep.
Fee Paid by Alfred Holt & Co.   Chest: Expansion 2   arr. 2. dep.
Report to " - by Birkton.   V. Capacity 33'   arr. 33' dep.
Previous School Forest Row Voluntary Primary.   Clinical N
Employer ___   Heart: T.T. 78 120 78 arr. 78 116 78 dep.
Previous Training Boy Scouts, 2 yrs.   Clinical N°
Intention for Future Alfred Holt - Steward   Fitness ✓   Spine ___
Watch Rodney.   Class Set: 1 __ 2 __ 3 __   Skin ___   Can / Cannot Swim

GENERAL REPORT. A cheerful boy, cooperative in a team, amenable to a team discipline and ready to help and be of service, but woefully afraid of testing physical conditions. His practical ability is fair, but could be improved by harder efforts, and he is completely confused when confronted with the unexpected. He requires good supervision to get conscientious effort from him, as his attention easily wanders, is very talkative with ready excuse for short comings, and tends to be easily influenced by poorer elements.
Nevertheless, friendly, likeable, and neat and clean.

Report on Bryan Wickens, part of Rodney watch, 1951

Going with the Flow..

I was working as an office junior in the fruit exchange in Victoria Street, and I wanted to go to sea.

So one dinner hour, I walked down Water Street and saw a huge brass nameplate with John Monks, Shipowners engraved on it.

A man with a captain's hat on, looked me up and down and said "You need more inches around your chest, lad, come back in six months".

So six months later, I went back, and was sent to the *"Vindicatrix"*, a merchant navy training ship in Gloucestershire.

Thousands of lads were trained there.

It was strict discipline. One of the things was being sent to stand under the clock, at the gatehouse, for hours.

On the river bank alongside the vessel, there was a toilet block - a trench dug in the ground, the length of the shed, with about 12 toilet slots.

One punishment would be to clean these out. Lads would only have a loincloth on.. and if the tide had not been in to clean the toilet channel out, they would have to get right down and push the stuff out.

Charles Boyd - Woolton

The Vindicatrix logo

"Vindi" boys. Ron Jones, first row, third right. Below. Charles Boyd, front row, far left, 1950

Out for the Count

I'd be fifteen or so, and I decided to join the Merchant Navy. I did my training on the *"Vindicatrix"*. I was a mother's boy, and that was a shock to the system.

The lads were from everywhere. Some of them were well-to-do, all thrown in together.

Quite a number had come from orphanages, and they were able to adapt better.

We were always starving. The food was terrible. My mother used to send me a store box, with all goodies in it, cake and sandwiches.

They used to come around at five o' clock in the morning with a cane, and you'd get hit, unbelievable, no pyjamas or anything, just an old grey blanket, and they'd whack you on the bare bottom to get up.

On deck, this is in January, they had a line of bowls with cold water in, that's how you'd get washed. Whatever came up after that, I could tackle it. But there were many who went over the wall.

On a Thursday night, for the Captain's entertainment, they'd get a boxing match going. If you committed a mis-demeanour, say you didn't do your bunk as it should be, any mortal

7

excuse, you had to fight for the Captain.

Gloves and all, no bantam or feather weight or anything, I was a weakling. I was about six stone, and they put me in with an Irish lad, who must have been about twelve stone. The skipper was there, and all the instructors, watching for blood - mine!

It was me who got tired, running around, and eventually I got caught with a blow that near took my head off. No expertise, you just tried to preserve yourself. I went down. I don't think I heard the count.

After I came to, I was informed that the skipper said I took a dive, and for that, I'd be on again next Thursday!

If you behaved yourself you used to get out, and we'd have a few goes at the Scrumpy, and come home singing.

Bill Sheridan -Netherton

Far Away Places...

My interest came with delivering baggage down to the liners and seeing these very ornate labels on all the cabin trunks, I was working for the railways then.

Joining in those days, you had to trail around all the shipping companies, literally hundreds of them, and ask for a job. You'd get the shake of the head.

I went to Canadian Pacific this one time, and they sent me to see the catering superintendent, and I was sent to the Liverpool Nautical Sea Training School. You started off as a boy rating, learning silver service, making bunks and that kind of thing.

It was known in the business as Dickie Bonds, a cook named Richard Bonds founded it.

Bruce Ferguson - Runcorn

The *Empress of France*

Going Down Down Down

As part of my training to be a sub-mariner, you had to go into a little compartment under a tank of water, and the drill was to open a valve and fill this little space. You had breathing apparatus on, and there was a hatch above you, once the pressure was equal, you opened that and went up, and that was your escape training. You had a little rubber mat in front of you to hold you from popping up too quick.

I couldn't swim.. in fact, when I joined, they asked me and I said "Why, have you no ships left?".

Mick Jones-Bootle

Submariners, Mick Jones, front centre. Note the 'Skull & Crossbones' being flown.

Fishing for Fags

In 1942 I came back to Liverpool and I was under a fellow named Wilkie, he was something to do with the Waif and Stray Society, and he boarded me out in Garston. I'd be about fourteen and half, and he got me a job on the Moyles boats. I was a deck boy there. They were port health medical boats and we'd take a doctor out to the ships coming in.

I was on her when all the Yanks were coming in. I can vouch for this, I remember one ship coming in, and when she docked at the quayside, she listed to one side, with the weight of all the troops on board lined up to get off. They were throwing cigarettes, and I had my bucket out, and my line, pulling all the cartons out of the water.

Arthur Burch - Woolton

Indentures

I was an apprentice deck officer, this was 1945, I fancied myself as Captain of the "*Queen Mary*".

I was with a company called James Nourse, they used to run out to the Persian Gulf and then on to India.

We used to pick up gunney sacks in Calcutta, take them round the Cape of Good Hope, across the Southern Atlantic, and into the West Indies. And the strange thing is, when I signed my indentures, I went to see my Grandfather who lived in Greasby. I was in awe of him, because he had a big white moustache, and I told him I was going to sea.

He asked me the name of the company. I said "James Nourse".

"Spell it", he said. Then he got up, without saying a word, and brought exactly the same indentures that he had signed with the same company.

The wages were exactly the same, too - he'd signed in 1885, something like that. I got £10 for the first year, £12 the second and then a big jump, to £18, £20 the fourth year.

Brian McEvoy-Wallasey

Dressing for Success

I used to interview the boys for jobs as commis waiters, from the Nautical Catering College. Mr. Brown used to send them across.

I had twenty five questions that they had to answer, and they were funny, you know, I'd say "Name three kinds of salad dressing"...and they'd say "Heinz, or Crosse and Blackwell," when what I wanted was "caesar" and "thousand island" instead.

They always came in with their aunty, never their mother, and I said to one little lad "You have a table for two on your station, two ladies together, which one do you seat first?" He looked and me and said "the prettiest". I used to say to all of them, "Keep your ears open and your mouth shut."

Jenny Kemp - Waterloo

Pennies for Lessons

I paid for my training at the Liverpool Nautical College with my tips from

when I was a telegram boy, and then I went away to sea.

Harry Hignett - Wallasey

Hungry all the time

I was two years in a home in Higher Bebington, St. Edmunds it was, my parents had split up, hence I was in the way. This was 1936. I was nearly twelve. It wasn't very pleasant at all, actually, you were hungry most of the time. For instance, you'd be saying your prayers before your evening meal and if you started laughing and giggling, messing about, the next thing was your bread and jam was gone. So that equipped me for when I went to sea in a coaster. I was fourteen then, only just over four feet tall.

Frank Walker - Wallasey

Ship Spotting

From eleven years old I wanted to go away to sea. I used to go down to the Pier Head with the books of all the shipping companies, and as the ships came in, I used to mark them down, ship spotting it was.

You had the big Cunard vessels and so on but they never appealed to me, it was tankers or the cargo ships that had the magic. You went round the world on those, crossing the Atlantic was just like a ferry.

I joined the Mersey Docks and Harbour Board first, and got a job on the floating crane "*Birkett*", as a deck boy in the galley. We used to go up and down the docks, loading, taking heavy loads off the ships. I used to take the ship's log book back to the dock board office, and then get the crew's messages, tea, sugar, stuff like that, and bring them back to the crane.

And of course the Overhead Railway was running then. They used to tell me which dock they'd be in, and I'd look out for the gib, sticking above the warehouses. Sometimes I'd judge the station right, sometimes I'd have a couple of quays to walk.

Dave Molyneux - Wallasey

Innocents Abroad

You had to have a medical at the Pool first, in the Sailors Home in Canning Place. This was 1945, you still had civilian identity cards, so I got some ink eradicator and changed my age. You had to be sixteen.

My first ship was the *"Samite"*, an American liberty ship, sailing to America. I was a "peggy" - and I think

years ago the job was given to someone who was wounded or disabled, and invariably they only had one leg - a "peg-leg" you see, that's how they got the name.

The firemen used to take me ashore and they'd go in a bar, and stick me in a milk bar with all these banana splits and milk shakes. The first thing I bought was a bunch of bananas, to take home to my mum - but when I got home they were rotten.

Bill Biddulph - Wallasey

Voyage of Discovery

I went to sea when I was sixteen, in 1946. My first trip was on board the *"Chrysanthemum"*, an old tramp.

What a voyage! She was a coal burner, and she broke down a lot, and the skipper started hitting the bottle. We ended up calling in at the Azores, for engine repairs, and when it came time to leave, the anchor got jammed and we lost it.

Merchant Navy Clothing Book, & overleaf, MN Clothing coupons, 1948.
Ron Jones

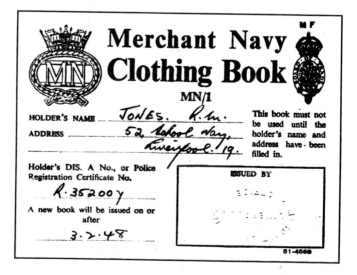

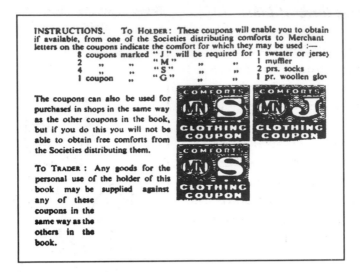

A few days later, the skipper went 'off his rocker' altogether, he was confined to his cabin by the the first mate who took over. We made it to Galveston, where we took on another skipper.

We set sail for Hamburg, picked the pilot up, and we ran aground. We were six weeks there, had to discharge most of the cargo in lighters, little barges, and then the tugs pulled her off the sand.

That was my first experience as a little deck boy.

Ronald Jones-Woolton

Slave Ship

I went to the shipping federation, this is about 1947, and they sent me to the *"Fort Slave"* - a good name for it, my first ship. She was a tramp, a Fort boat that had been built in Canada, you know, during the lease-lend.

I was a deck boy. I was what they called the "Peggy" - looked after the lads.

I'd be scrubbing out and being sick at the same time. The crew said "Listen, son, when you get home, go back to your mother because you'll never make a sailor".

Bill Sheridan-Netherton

Flushed with success

I remember being in Columbo, you don't go alongside there, and the monsoon broke, and our stern line broke. We were just swinging around. The engineers were working on the engines.

We four apprentices got into a lifeboat and rowed to the stern of the ship, they lowered a line, and we had to leap onto the buoy, from the boat, to secure her. I did this, and I felt terribly important, but as I was climbing back up the rope ladder, full of myself, someone on board flushed the toilet, and of course it came out of the side, all over me.

Brian McEvoy-Wallasey

The lowest form of Life

My great grandfather was a Master of one of the Boston tea clippers. I remember seeing pictures of the great liners and thinking that's really what I want to do.

In 1950, I went to sea as an apprentice officer with Cunard White Star as it was then. I was sixteen, and basically the lowest form of life on board. She was called the *"Arabia"*, a cargo ship, they had a very big cargo fleet in those days.

I was indentured to the company, my parents paid £50, you did everything from painting the top of the mast to scrubbing the bilges.

Robin Woodall - Hoylake

LIST OF OFFICERS

Captain—W. M. STEWART, O.B.E.

Chief Engineer .... R. DUNCAN	Chief Officer...H. A. STONEHOUSE, D.S.C., R.D., R.N.R.
Surgeon.......... H. M. H. ASHWIN, M.R.C.S., L.R.C.P.	Purser....................A. GRAHAM
Chief Steward..............A. LEWIS	Tourist Purser...... T. S. HAMILTON
Tourist Steward ...... C. BAKEWELL	

Every picture tells a story

I remember my first ship, the *"Anchises"* sailing to the Far East, and one of the memorable things, an oddi ty you might say, was a very nice man who had twenty seven abbreviated girls' names on the lower portion of his protruding anatomy, and on each thigh he had a tattoo of a girl, so whichever side he dressed, one had hold of it! The older men would advise you, in my case there were three deck boys in one cabin, and if any seamen were to come in your room, within a minute, someone would come and tell them to get out. We were protected.

Stan Amos - Moreton

Voices in the Night

My Dad had been a Blue Funnel man, and one of the traits I inherited from him is insomnia.

Now, Blue Funnel was renowned for their motor sirens, everyone knew them, they didn't hoot, they had a deep deep roar, a beautiful sound. Dad would be in bed, in the front room, with Mum and I'd be in my back bedroom, and we'd hear this roar of a Blue Funnel ship calling the tugs to attention in Vittoria Dock. And Dad would shout through: " Are you awake, son? There's the *"Prometheus"* going"... "Yes, dad".

And then, later on, you'd hear the three blasts in the Vittoria basin, "She's going astern, son, now". "Yes, Dad".

Then finally, you'd hear six blasts when she was dismissing the tugs, she was on her way.

It wasn't a source of annoyance, it was a bond.

And that was the feeling, a father could talk to his son at midnight about a ship as if it was one of the family. And all the port was the same.

Colin Sharp - Bromborough

A Blue Funnel match book

Chapter Two: For those in Peril

The "*Bismarck*" haunts my dreams now
With bodies floating on the sea
Much the sorrow and much the suffering
Before we saw victory

Merseyside of course was the hub of operations for the Battle of the Atlantic, and many local families were touched by tragedies at sea. This chapter includes stories of extreme bravery, with memories of the *"Lancastria"* from two of the very few survivors, as well as a first hand account of the *"Thetis"* disaster.

Salvage vessel SS *Ranger-* involved in *Thetis* submarine disaster, 1939.

A gentleman's war

We were on our way back from Brazil, on the *"Dictator"*, this would be about 1915, loaded with sugar.

We called into Las Palmas, and loaded the decks with crates of bananas.

Sunday morning, couple of hundred miles south west of the Scillies, I heard a shell go over, and there's a submarine, half submerged, about half a mile away. I told the mate "She's got flags, up, sir". So we swung the lifeboats out, I had my boots in my hand, and my coat, I'd torn the lining out and I'd up somehow, to make themselves look like a sailing ship in the distance. I always say it was the U120 but then they said it was U20. It was in April that same year he got the *"Lusitania"*.

We were hanging on to a ring bolt of the submarine, and the young commander, he spoke perfect English, said he'd tow us clear of the crates of bananas. He towed us two miles. He told us he'd already sunk one sailing ship, and two merchant boats.

William Tennant -Bootle

Advert from World War One… 'A Gentleman's war'

stuffed it with bananas.

The submarine Captain waited for us to clear, and then he torpedoed her. The ship wouldn't sink, so they fired shells into her, you could see the holes, you know. I suppose the sugar had set like concrete. Then down she went.

In those war days, subs used to rig a sail

Thetis

I joined the *"Ranger"* in Liverpool, she used to be berthed in Albert Dock. She was the salvage vessel for the Liverpool and Glasgow Salvage Company. My uncle was superintendent with the company. I was on her for

SS *"Ranger"* and Naval Salvage vessel HMS "*Tedworth*" working on raising *"Thetis"*

Diver working on "Thetis" rescue

a while, and then they had this old coal boat, come from Newcastle, called the *"Zelo"* and she was built with wooden bollards on her, with 4 inch wires. We riggers lived on the after deck in rough accommodation. We had to get the wire ropes ready to sling.

We were getting about ten shillings a day then, big money.

We had a couple of divers, Freddie Winchester was one, they would go down and when low water came, the stern of the "*Thetis*" would come up. My uncle Jimmy wanted to cut a hole in the stern and put an escape hatch in, at that time we didn't know there were over 100 people inside. He thought he could have saved them but the Navy would not allow it, they were under the impression that she would come to the surface. But her bow was stuck in the sand bar. At every high water, she'd go down again, and that went on for weeks.

The people in the engine room were tapping, S.O.S., the divers heard them. Only four escaped.

We were trying to get her up and these four inch wires snapped, so we had to go back to Cammell Lairds, and they put steel bollards on deck and had nine inch wire, specially made. A hell of a

Diving Bell on board
ss "*Zelo*"

Mick Sheehan (right),
Jimmy Donovan
(centre) and diver.
The salvaging
of Submarine HMS
Thetis

job to get these under the sub. The divers would go down and put a smaller wire under, then we'd be on deck, hauling up, four inch, six inch, nine inch wires. It took a long time and she only had so much time for the tide to lift her.

It would take a couple of days to secure one wire. We had to keep tightening the wires with "handy billies".

And then she'd be towed towards shore, and once the tide changed, she dropped again.

The first body they got up was a stoker, they put him in a boat with the diver. The bodies were all bloated and as soon as you touched them they burst. We had no gas masks or nothing, and I had never smoked in my life til then. They kept putting cigarettes in my mouth to keep the smell away. We eventually got her on the beach.

Mick Sheehan - Canada

A new name

I sailed in convoy bound for the Middle East in March, 1941, on the RMS *"Strathallan"* - a P & O ship. I watched the city and the buildings and the Wallasey coast until they faded on the horizon. I did not return 'til August 1945.

I remember seeing the repaired and re-commissioned *"Thetis"*, she was re-named *"Thunderbolt"*, in dock in Alexandria in Egypt, in November 1941. I went on board, and it really was rather eerie to imagine how terri-ble it must have been to be trapped down there. She was later sunk in the war.

Jim Rehill - Allerton

All the little ships

I joined the RNVR in the Salthouse Dock in 1938. When war broke out, we were called up, and we were so fed up filling sandbags, that when they asked for volunteers to go on Merchant ships, some of us went.

We were put on coasters that went from Newcastle to Southend. We were to protect vessels, and that's where the name comes in, Defensively Equipped Merchant Ships (DEMS).

You had two lines of ships going down the East Coast, planes used to machine gun us, U boats used to tie up at the buoys, and as you came abreast, they'd let go a couple of torpedoes. Each ship had a gunner on - only one, so they called old men back to teach the mer-chant seaman all about gunnery.

But then again, I've been on ships with 40 gunners, because they started put-ting Bofors guns on.

We went to Dunkirk on one of the Isle of Man boats, the *"Tynwald"*, five times we went. We sailed from Dover,

sent down from Liverpool.

All you could see was all the place, afire. We were dive bombed, but we opened up on them. There were six-teen of us from Liverpool on the guns. Not one of them complained.

The pier was under bombardment, but we still got them on board, and as soon as we had about a thousand on, away we'd go.

Harold Watkins-Runcorn

D.E.M.S. Gunners logo

21

One man's war

I was 24, when war broke out. I enlisted in the army, and then volunteered for the Merchant Navy, because we thought we'd get merchant navy pay! They also got £10 a month danger money. Greed for gold!

Two days after, I was taken to T.J.Hughes, issued with civilian clothes, and I sailed from Cammell Lairds on the *"Athol Foam"*. I was a gunner on board, in the DEMS.

We sailed for about fifteen days in a convoy of about twenty two ships, eighteen were sunk including my ship which was sunk by shellfire. A lot of the lifeboats were broken so I held onto wreckage.

The *Scharnhorst,* she came and picked us up. They were very good to us, the Captain was not a Nazi... We were taken back to Brest, then in cattle trucks, you know, like the wagons they used to take Jews, for about seven days, to a prison camp in Poland, and then to a factory on the Polish border. It had been an American factory before the war. We were digging trenches for water pipes.

The toilets there were a forty foot piece of plank, with holes in, full of maggots. Food was three boiled potatoes, a cup of soup, and five men to a loaf. I was there for two years and nine months...'til the Russians broke through.

They marched us, from the 19th January 1945 to 25th April, fifteen hundred of us, to Museberg in Austria. We were liberated by General Patton. I've been lucky all my life.

Bill Citrine - Halewood

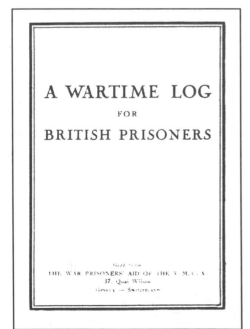

Front Page of Log for British POWs, World War II

Drawing of camp (unknown) by British POW (unknown)

No choice

My first voyage - my only voyage - was four years on Russian convoys.
I saw a lot of awful things, we lost ships every convoy.
I remember one particular time, this ship was torpedoed, and they were all in the water, full of oil and freezing, and I thought our skipper was going to pick them up - I'll never forget it as long as I live - but what he did, there was a U boat down below and he went right through the survivors, and depth charged the sub. He kept going around and around, depth charging, making sure. But if we stopped, we would have been torpedoed ourselves.

Tommy Clark-Runcorn

Just a boy

Because I wasn't yet sixteen, C.P.R. wouldn't let me sail anymore, with the war on and that, so I went on the *"Automedon"*, Blue Funnel, going out to the Far East. This was September 1940. We were on our way to Penang, and we were intercepted by a raider, the *"Atlantis"*. We took a good pounding with shells. I was watching on the after end, everything cascading around me, even the awning. I never got a scratch. The bridge was smashed. Everyone up there was killed apart from the QM. The lifeboats were blown away, the funnel was like a colander. I tried to look after the Chief Steward, he was a right mess, most of his guts blown away.
The Germans came on board, and they looted the ship. They took cigarettes, food, whisky, all sorts off the ship. They got a magic haul too, they got all the documents, intact, every little bit of information about the security of Singapore. No one knows why all that was on board, but the Commander in Chief in Malaya had come over to London, and had a war cabinet meeting. He went back on a cruiser, and we

AUTOMEDON

"Automedon"

above: Sinking of the *"Automedon"*, taken from*"Atlantis"*. Below: Sand Bostal POW camp, Stalag 10B.
Over: Lavatories, Marlag und Milag Nord POW camp and Red Cross Christmas Card

took all the intelligence. We didn't know about that until afterwards.

Then they put charges on, and a torpedo, and finished her off. We were put on board a Norwegian tanker that they'd taken. Conditions were appalling, we were battened down for nearly three months in the hold. Sleeping on the mooring ropes. They used to lower water in barrels for drinking or wiping yourself down. Lavatories - well, virtually none existent. You just found somewhere, used buckets and slopped them into a big barrel and they'd haul that out. Food was one thin slice of bread a day, and soup like water.

We eventually got cattle trucked into German, Stalag 10B at Sand Bostal... we were in one corner of that camp, with the RN chaps. When they brought all the Russian POWs in, there must have been 8000 men there. A lot of the Russians died, but the men kept their bodies propped up in the huts, so they'd be counted, and still get their rations. But the Germans cottoned on

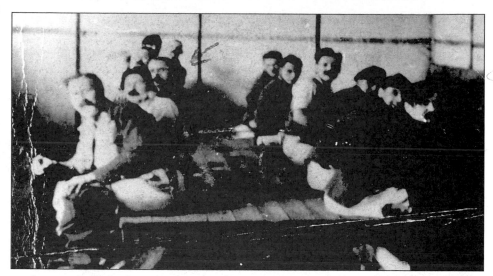

to that, and we had to drag them out and bury them.

I was there about six months and there was an outbreak of typhus and the Red Cross made them move us out, us Merchant men and the RN boys, about three thousand, a hell of a lot from the Liverpool area. The second camp was Marlag und Milag. I was there til the end of the year, a lot of the lads went home in 1943, on an exchange, but I was on punishment, so I missed out.

I was always in trouble, on punishment party at lot. I'd have to take the "smelly nellies" - a long tank on wheels, all the urine and everything from you know where sucked up and I'd be between these shafts, running along, like a horse and cart, and then you'd open it out and spread it on the fields.

I worked on the peat party when I was in Stalag B, stacking them to dry them out in a pyramid, and I thought "blow it", pulled a couple out, got inside and fell asleep. Woke up, no one around, and I went back to the camp. I was

Best Wishes for a Happy Return Home
from :-

AUSTRALIAN RED CROSS
BRITISH RED CROSS & ST. JOHN
CANADIAN RED CROSS
INDIAN RED CROSS & ST. JOHN AMBULANCE ASSOCIATION
JOINT COUNCIL OF ST. JOHN AND RED CROSS OF NEW ZEALAND
SOUTH AFRICAN RED CROSS

We Salute You and wish you the very
Best of Luck.

hungry. The guards shouted at me to go away, they didn't realise I was a prisoner. I didn't get punished for that. In Marlag und Milag, I slipped out between the main gate and the post, because I was so small, and was gone two days, starving and wet. I went to a farm, and the old man pedalled off to let the camp know. They put me on the "wire" for three days, standing at attention all day.

When I got home at the end of the war, the Blue Funnel sent me to Summerlands, the Merchant Navy place near Kendal.

That was wonderful, it was like a luxury hotel, tennis courts, great food, bike rides. Brilliant. I was there a month.

Frank Walker-Wallasey

All the nice girls..

I was an ordinary seaman in the Royal Navy, proper bell bottoms and that, pill box hat with HMS *"Destroyer"* on it and that...the girls used to make us laugh, they used to come and touch our dickie, like.. that was your collar.

I went down near Plymouth for my training, It was May 1940 and it took me two days to get there.

Our rifle drill was with broom sticks, we had no rifles, our boat drill was a boat on trestles, off the ground, and you had to row in mid air.

The first vessel I sailed on was the *"Duchess of Richmond"*, and we sailed from Liverpool to Canada to pick up one of the yankee lease/lend destroy-

ers, HMS *"Burnham"*. They weren't really built for the Atlantic, more for coastal waters. All the port holes were riveted, and when you were in your bunk, you could see water trickling down. I did nineteen crossings of the Atlantic.

We were on two bob a day, the Canadians were on five times as much and the Yanks, seven times as much. In Iceland, they had separate pubs for the English and the Yanks, with guards outside, because no matter where we docked, we always left someone behind in hospital.

I saw Victor Mature in Iceland, you should have seen the medals on his chest, it was laughable.

When we first went to America, as soon as we got to the dock gates, there were hundreds of American women waiting there, they'd be fighting, shouting for us to you come home with them, you'd be pulled to bits, they'd drag you off to a car, and look after you, entertain you.

But when America came into the war, the tune was very very different "What are you Limey b......s doing over here, and our lads are over there, fighting your war?"

Peter Johnson-Seaforth

Crew of HMS *"Burnham"* - part of photograph
obscured for reasons of national security.

Danger money

I was nineteen when I joined the navy, I did three months training in Butlins in Pwllheli and then joined the *"Etrib"* bound for Gibraltar.

It took us twenty one days, through gunboat alley. On the way back, I was in one of the three ships that were hit, the *"Pallayo"*, the *"Samdol"* and ours.

I had managed to get up through a scuttle with the others and the first bloke I bumped into was Billy Swinchin. It was as black as coal, this night, all the midships was gone, it was broke in half, and Billy said to me, "Come on Joe, over the side, or we're going to go down with this boat", so we went over. We lost one another. Billy was unfortunate, he had seventy five days adrift, but suddenly this corvette the *"Marigold"* appeared out of nowhere. . I scrambled up the nets and got on board and away we went, but there were still blokes in the water.

In the Med. if they went beyond a certain degree east or west, they finished up on danger money, the Merchant service, they were on much better pay than the RN. I did some of the North African landings, and if the MN went beyond a particular place, they got their danger money.

We went back to Algiers, and picked German prisoners up, two trips of 16 days. We used to pull up at the Pier Head and of all things they used to be loaded on Pickfords furniture vans, full of German prisoners.

I was also in Doolally, it's not a "nut house", it was in the first world war, but later it was a big homeward bound trooping dept. I was there after VJ day, in a draft of fifty matelots waiting for transport home, and I think we'd be there yet but bubonic plague broke out in the surrounding area and we were told if anyone caught it, we'd be in quarantine there for nine months.

We were brought down to Bombay and onto the *"Isle De France"*.

She was a beautiful ship, I've never seen anything like it, she had a church with a vaulted roof that went through three decks, they'd left that, not touched it, even though it was a troop ship.

Joseph Jeffries-Warrington

Silent Nights

My sister in law's husband, Billy Swinchin, was on the Moss Hutchinson ship, the *"Etrib"* that was lost in June 1942, and Billy got onto a raft, by himself. It was provisioned for twenty eight men, what they call iron rations, enough to sustain you, biscuits and water in tanks. He drifted, lost all track of time, completely on his own.

In the end he ran out of food, just had water. He drifted in and out of a coma almost, and he woke up to the smell of onions. He did not remember being picked up.

He found himself on board a German submarine. The captain asked him which ship he'd been on. He checked and came back to Billy and said "Little Englander, I tell you, you are amazing. You've been 75 days adrift". The crew,

ABANDONING SHIP

Wireless messages and equipment

Find out if an S.O.S. has been sent out from the ship, and if an answer has been received.

See that the ship's portable wireless transmitter and receiving set are taken into a boat. Remember that they can easily be damaged if dropped; therefore *pass* them into the boat; if you have to drop them, they are less likely to be damaged if dropped into the water, as they are buoyant and, for a time at any rate, will remain watertight.

Instruments, nautical tables and charts

Take your sextant and nautical tables with you in the lifeboat. Special water-proofed charts of the oceans of the world are being issued, showing details of the prevailing winds and currents like those given in the American Hydrographical Charts. If you have already had yours, take them with you.

Clothing

Take waterproof clothing (oilskins, seaman's protective suit, anti-gas cape, or mackintosh) and gather up any extra warm clothing, blankets or Duffel coats. Experience has shown only too often that unnecessary suffering has been caused by lack of clothing when in a boat. Even in the tropics it may feel bitterly cold at night. It is better to carry too much clothing than too little, for it will protect you not only against the cold, but also against the sun. Do not imagine that the weight of this extra clothing will be a danger to you in the water. Modern lifebelts will support a person in the water fully dressed and wearing sea boots. Carry a pair of dry socks in your pocket, in a waterproof package.

Extra water

Water is more important than food; it is of such great importance that you should **make every effort to take** extra water with you. Improvise containers wherever possible: 40 gallon oil drums can be used; they are easily cleaned and sterilised by steam in the engine room; they should be painted white; *half-filled* with drinking water and stowed on the upper deck ready to float off or be rolled overboard. Fill and take with you water-bottles or similar containers (preferably not of glass). Masters who have appreciated the paramount importance of an adequate water supply have succeeded in improvising stowage for as much as 120 gallons per boat.

Food

You are unlikely to need more food than is stored in the lifeboat, and no extra food should be taken at the expense of extra water and extra clothing. Extra water is of much greater value than extra food.

Release of life-saving appliances

All life-saving appliances should be released, even if they are not needed immediately. The water and stores they contain are valuable and may be picked up later. Gear should be transferred from boats which are damaged or cannot be lowered.

Going Overboard

If you do not get away in a boat, go over the lower side if the ship has listed. If you go over the upper side you will be in danger of being badly hurt by barnacles and marine growths, and of fracturing your ankles by hitting your heels against the bilge keel. When the lower side of the listed vessel happens also to be the weather side take care to avoid being washed back on board, and in this case, if possible, take to the water from the bow or stern, whichever is the lower. Jump into the water feet first; do not dive.

If fuel oil has been discharged into the sea, you should avoid contact with it as far as possible. If you have to jump into the sea, hold your nose. If you have to swim through a patch of oil, keep your head and eyes high and your mouth closed (oil on the surface makes this easier by calming the sea). If you swallow fuel oil, it

Extract on 'Abandoning Ship"...taken from 'A Guide to the Preservation of Life at Sea after Shipwreck'. Issued by the Medical Research Council, 1943.

because they were seamen, were thrilled at his bravery, they spoon fed him. But he was five weeks a prisoner on that submarine, during that time they were looking for our ships.

He ended up in a prison of war camp eventually. He spent three years there. Within four weeks of getting home, he was back at sea.

Since then I've met a man who was in the camp with Billy. He said they were put onto a farm to work, it was Christmas and someone said Billy could play the accordion, and so he played in the village school, "Silent Night" and all that, and everyone was crying.

Theresa Bassett-Aigburth

A Sundodger's tale

I joined HMS P42, she later became HMS *"Unbroken"*, because Churchill ordered, in 1942, that all submarines must be named. The rest of the navy called us "Sundodgers". We were supposed to be "underhand, ", "underwater", and "damned un-English", but I thought we were the cream!

I was an Asdic operator, it's called sonar now, you listened for the screws of ships and you'd hear "ping, ping".

We joined the Flotilla at Malta. Our skipper, told us "We are the opening batsmen of the Second 11", they always used cricketing terminology! We were taking secret agents to the South of France, one of them was Captain Peter Churchill, who married Odette, the George Cross woman.

Mick Jones, aged 18, on becoming a Submariner.

He used to walk around at night and talk to us. Before they were landed, they were sitting sewing French tabs inside their shirts, nothing was left to chance. The night before they landed, Churchill was taking a swig from a little flask, and the ward room mess man asked him what it was, and Captain Churchill said "It's brandy, but it's laced with something to keep me awake for 48 hours."

I remember August 1942, it was the Malta convoy, to relieve the seige. We were patrolling off the North East coast of Sicily. The convoy took a hell of a hammering, I think only three ships out of twenty three reached Malta...it was carnage.

We got a signal that there was an Italian task force coming our way...four cruisers and eight destroyers. The skipper said he was going to attack and we thought "Oh Christ", there's only us. Anyhow, he went in,

Mick Jones, extreme left front, standing, Fort Blockhouse, Gosport, July 1941

under the destroyer screen. We fired four torpedoes. We badly damaged two cruisers. The skipper got an immediate DSO for that.

They started depth charging then - 119 altogether - that was one of my jobs, to record every explosion. Put it this way, I didn't need any Beechams pills. It's an eric feeling, to hear a destroyer rushing over the top of you - everyone in the boat could hear those pings bouncing around.

And then you wait for the bangs.

Mick Jones -Bootle

Boy Gunner

We were on the "*Windsor Castle*", a Union Castle Line ship, taking troops to North Africa, about 50 miles off Algiers, in convoy,

I was on the Oerlikon gun, with sixty rounds of ammunition. We were trained for it by the DEMS gunners, I had just two days training. I was sixteen then, just a deck boy. I had a steward in the gun nest with me, he was the loader.

The night we were torpedoed, we heard a plane go over, but nobody opened fire. It circled round, we took no notice, thought it must be one of ours. So I said to the steward, "I'll go down and fill the teapot with cocoa".

Anyway, I was just putting the lid on the teapot when the blast came, and I smelled cordite, but I didn't realise that it was a torpedo.

All the lights went out, and then I knew. I found my way onto deck,

George Baker's ID card for New York

The Union Castle boat - *'Windsor Castle'*

everyone was in a panic and the Captain was shouting "Abandon ship". She wasn't actually going down, just settling; some troops were jumping over the side, some were throwing rafts over, one of the nurses jumped between the side of the ship and a destroyer was coming alongside to pick people up off deck. She was crushed between the ship and the destroyer.

I was in the doctor's lifeboat. Everyone was shouting "Pick me up" but we couldn't, we'd have been overloaded. We waited, put the sea anchor out, and when I looked around, we saw a Jacob's ladder on the side of the ship, so we went back on. The shop had been blown out and there were dollar bills all over the place. We never touched a thing.

We went to see if we could help, but we couldn't. So we got back to the lifeboat and waited. About eight in the morning, a destroyer came and picked us up, took us to Algiers.

Two tugs went out to tow her back, but she turned turtle, and they had to let go quick.

I had thirty days survivors leave.

George Baker-Bootle

MERCHANT NAVY A/A GUNNERY COURSE.

CERTIFICATE OF PROFICIENCY.

Date Stamp of Training Centre.

Name .... G........l

Rank or Rating .... Deckboy

B. of T. or D.B. No. ....

has completed the Merchant Navy A/A Gunnery Course and is qualified in the firing and cleaning and oiling of * ALL _ _ _ 'S AND _ _ CES

_ _ _ IN D.E.M.S.

Rank .... COMMANDER.

D.E.M.S. Training Centre .... GLASGOW

* Insert type of guns _ _ _ ALONE IS ONLY _ _ _ _ ATION THEN

(799) Wt. 11104/P6007 50m 8/43 C.B.& E.Ltd. Gp. 671. [over

Certificate of Proficiency, Merchant Navy A/A Gunnery Course. George Baker

What price valour?

War broke out when I was on my first voyage, on the "*Antonia*", so we went down to Nova Scotia to sail home in convoy. They put a gun on the aft end, but it was made of wood, to scare the planes off!

My next mission was to France, on the "*Lancastria*", to get the troops back. We were making big "doggies" (pans) of scouse for them, they were starving. We had a few scares and then the bells started going, and there was this almighty thump, a bomb had dropped on the foreward hatch. You could hear "Abandon ship, every man for himself", then there was another almighty "doings", and a bomb went down the funnel. I made for the after end. Everyone was rushing around but no panic, she was going down then, the bow was sinking. A couple of us were getting the hatch boards off and throwing them over, as rafts, you see.

I had a life jacket, you know, the old cork ones and there was a soldier next to me, he couldn't swim, so I gave him my life jacket, because I was a good swimmer. There was a lot of oil being spewed out…men were shouting, "get clear, get clear, you'll get sucked under". We saw legs, arms, we saw a lot of stuff I can't talk about.

We got the injured onto the rafts, pushing away from the ship, we were exhausted.

We watched her go down, men still clambering down the side, Captain Sharp and the officers actually walked off. It took her about twenty minutes to go down…quietly.

The sea was full of dead fish and bombs were still dropping around us..

There was one destroyer in the bay, she was firing away, men were swimming for her, but her propellers were going on and off, and some of them were churned up, we could hear the screaming. It was was awful.

Next thing, I was picked up by a small trawler and they took us to the "*John Holt*. They landed us in Plymouth.

We walked to the workhouse, well, it was a hospital then. They had mattresses on the floor and they gave us a mug of tea and a big cheese butty.

Next morning, after breakfast, we were told to pick clothes out from a big pile they'd collected from the people of Plymouth. I ended up with a pair of trousers covered in paint, a jumper with holes in and a pair of pumps. A Cunard man gave us a sandwich and a ten bob note for the journey.

When we got to Lime Street, there were dozens of women, in shawls, waiting for news asking us " Hey lad, have you seen so and so?"

Next day, I went down to the Cunard and my money had stopped from the day we were bombed. Not only that, though, they wanted to take the ten shillings back off us.

Andrew Lockett-Maghull

Never Volunteer

I was about to be shipped home on the "*Lancastria*", but I volunteered to take tanks up to Arras, instead. They used

33

to stay "Never volunteer for any-thing", but I reckon that saved my life…

The "Lancastria" was out in the bay, not in port, and the troops were ferried out to her. I learned later that she'd been sunk, they still don't know exactly how many were killed.

I came home on one of the last two vessels to leave, she was about the size of one of the Mersey ferries and just before I got on board, I found two metal boxes on the quayside, full of cigarettes, so I gave them out to the lads for the journey home to Blighty.

I received a telegram saying that Stan was missing, presumed killed. We didn't have a clue what was going on then. He came home in the June, tattered and torn, no uniform or anything. We had no idea about the "Lancastria" or what a lucky escape he'd had, because Churchill kept it all quiet, he was a very crafty man!

Stan and Ann Bennion, Kirkby

A quartermaster's tale

I joined the "Lancastria", signed on in Cunard Building, as quartermaster. I knew where she was going, I didn't care. Arrived in Plymouth the following day. We got orders to go to St. Nazaire.

It was four o 'clock in the morning, I'd just come off the wheel, a beautiful summer's morning. A flock of German bombers came from the east, and they dropped bombs. The "Franconia" got damaged and she then left.

We anchored about 5 miles off the port of St. Nazaire, about seven in the morning. HMS "Highlander" came out to us- she was loaded down with troops, children, women, dogs and cats and God knows what…They were flocking aboard. I was off watch then 'til 12 o'clock. Tugs came out and other destroyers, and we were being attacked all the time, but no bombs were dropped on us.

I went on watch, down the gangway, the quartermaster's always on when the gangway is out. We had a dozen or so stewards showing the survivors where to go, I was checking, with a stop watch or something, how many was coming aboard. Trying to keep an estimate. They were six or ten or twelve to a cabin, and by that time, around 2pm, my mate relieved me and I went on the bridge, standing by the wheel in case we got orders.

The Chief Officer was there, Mr. Grattidge, the First Officer, Mr. Roberts, and Captain Sharp.

By that time we had well over five thousand on board aboard, there were more than a thousand airforce men in the foreward hatch. Troops laying on the deck, all dead beat, jerry planes were coming over, machine gunning the decks, they were just targets.They were after the bridge, too.

They got the "Oransay", a direct hit on the bridge. She was about a quarter of a mile away.

We were still loading. The Captain was asking "Where am I going to put them? We're way over". But the army guys insisted on taking more on board,

Winston Churchill on board unknown vessel, 16th July 1942

and the Captain looked at the Chief Officer and said "Well, there's nothing we can do, but when I leave here, I want an escort".

That was about twenty five to three.

The Captain asked me to get the estimate of how many were on board. I went down, and I think it was the second mate said we had well over seven thousand, not including the crew of four hundred and forty nine.

I went down then to the crew's quarters to tell the QM is was time to relieve me, seven bells, when the first bomb dropped down No.2 hatch. That's where all the airforce guys were. The concussion blew me all the way up the scuttle thirty or forty yards. The storekeeper was lying on top of the hatch, he'd been hit with machine gun fire. I was never so cool in my life as that day, I told the troops to move him, lay him on deck. There was a machine gun there, I grabbed it and fired at the planes coming over.

Then I went back up to the bridge.

Then on the next attack, three of them machine gunned the bridge and Mr. Roberts got killed, and I was talking to the Chief, we ducked behind the rail. I can see the Captain now by the wheelhouse door. The ship went over to the starboard side. A bomb went down the funnel, next was on the tourist deck, third on the after deck. At the same time, the machine gunners were everywhere.

Lifeboats got jammed. Troops were trying to get the women and children aboard. The Captain had been shouting for the troops to go to the port side, so the boats could be levelled off, you had thousands of troops swinging from one side to the other, she went onto her port side. But then you couldn't lower anything, she was too high. I was in the water by that time, I'd cut my clothes off with a sea knife, and I got on a hatch board, two army guys with me, I told them keep kicking or the suction would take us.

We got away a couple of hundred

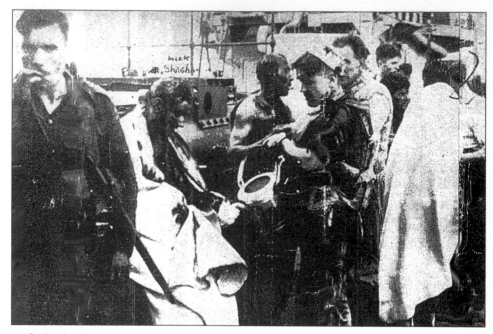

Mick Sheehan, wrapped in blanket, on board HMS "*Highlander*"

yards, machine guns firing at us, bombs, oil everywhere. We were full of oil...I turned around, saw her go down in 21 minutes.

We were there for hours. Lot of people were killed in the water, hundreds. The army guys drifted away, I think the machine guns got them, and sometime after, getting dusk, I was cold, HMS "*Highlander*" arrived. I was scooped up, I was naked, slippery, full of oil. They got me on board, boy, did I feel good then. One of the navy guys gave me a blanket and a cup of rum or hot cocoa, put life back in me.

I was transferred to the *John Holt* ship, up rope ladders. There were hundreds already there, badly wounded. But I seen sights on the "*Lancastria*" when that first bomb went off, fellows with their heads blown off, legs, everything. ...Indescribable.

I ended up going home to Old Swan with just women's bloomers and a jacket on. My first stop was the Red House.

Mick Sheehan-Canada

Distressed British Seamen

I signed up, you see, came home and my mother said "Did you get in the navy?" and I said "Oh, better than that, the money's £29 a month, or something like that". "Have you seen today's paper?" she said, "Twenty six ships out of fifty sunk in one convoy". That was my introduction to the Merchant Navy.

I was on the "*Oronsay*" and when we got to Capetown, the powers that be decided that it was so comfortable in the South Atlantic, they could send us singly instead of in convoy, so we had

36

to zig zag every ten minutes, doing 18 knots, and then this Italian submarine hit the engine room. Now I think he must have been a nice chap because he stood by. The ship listed to one side, so on the starboard side, we could get the lifeboats away, I was engaged in lowering the lifeboats, we only had about three hundred and sixty people on board including two women, one was a diamond merchant's daughter and the other was a nurse.

We got away, stood off, I got the impression that he waited 'til we were all off, this Italian, and then he put another one in, it took four torpedoes to sink her...I saw her go down, stern first.

Once we got in the lifeboat, it was absolutely crammed. There were about 36 in the boat and I was the only sailor. We had ropes from one boat to another, started off with thirteen, until we hit a very bad night, the ropes broke and when we woke next morning, five of the boats had disappeared. I found out later that they were eventually picked up by a French vessel, landed at Dakar and interned.

We were 500 miles off land. I was in that boat for eight days. Conditions were terrible, your bottom was sore, food - two biscuits with pemmican - a meat substitute, scraped off and on, two Horlicks tablets and that was it. Water ran out, but fortunately it rained, we put a piece of a sail and caught water, but the sail was bright orange and so was the water. It was horrible. I sucked a button .

We finally got rescued, HMS "*Brilliant*" wasn't very big, so it was crowded. The following day, she was running out of fuel, and they had to burn paint to get us into port, and suddenly the ship lurched to one side. The signal sounded for "take your stations" and then the boat righted itself.

The problem had been that these two ladies who'd been rescued had been equipped with clothing, and they were standing silhouetted against the sun. It was parachute silk, their figures could be seen through it, and all these poor distressed British seaman, supposed to be dying of exposure, had all crowded to one side of the ship to see these sil houettes!

Thomas Taylor- Stockton Heath

Attracting attention : A strict lookout should be kept from the boat at all times. Do not be extravagant with your red flares, smoke signals or rockets, as their number is limited. They should be under the immediate control of an officer, who should see they are not used wastefully. If an aircraft is seen or heard in the vicinity, wait until it is heading in your direction before you fire a rocket or flare, and remember that you can hear an aircraft long before you can see it. Remember, too, that you can see an aircraft some time before its occupants are likely to see you; do not, therefore, fire your rocket or flare until it is fairly close to you. Be prepared to fire a second rocket or flare to confirm your first.
If you have no rockets nor flares, you can often make yourself conspicuous to aircraft by churning up the sea with oars or paddles. If you possess a W/T set do not run it down by sending out frequent signals, for the battery has only a short life. The watertight battery, supplied with the set, is designed to last for 48 hours automatic intermittent sending. Make sure the instrument is correctly tuned to suit the aerial used. If practicable, transmit S 0 S's during international distress periods, the times of which are 15-18 minutes and 45-48 minutes past each hour G.M.T.; distress signals are more likely to be picked up during these periods.(Extract from 'A Guide to the Preservation of Life at Sea after Shipwreck' 1943)

Minding Your Own Business

My first submarine was HMS "*Sunfish*" everything was cluttered, no room for niceties - you slept where you could, on a table or anything like that, there were no bunks.

When you were at sea, water had to be conserved, so every four days, you got a bucket of soapy water, you'd go down to the engine room and about four of you would share that bucket.

Lavatories - they were suicidal contraptions. There was a lever alongside the pan, an air bottle beside you and a depth gauge beside you, and to blow all your waste out, you needed a pressure of 45lbs. So you charged the air bottle up and then went through the routine of pushing the lever forward, bringing it back to neutral, and then you pushed it back to "blow". That supposedly blew everything out but you could make mistakes, and you could get a "flashback".. you got your own back!

Before you did the "blow", there was phone there, and you had to ask the control room for permission to blow the after head. If it was rough up top, you'd get permission, but if it was calm, you couldn't have bubbles coming up and giving the game away, so you left it for the next man. There was a lot of constipation on that sub because people were reluctant to go!

Mick Jones-Bootle

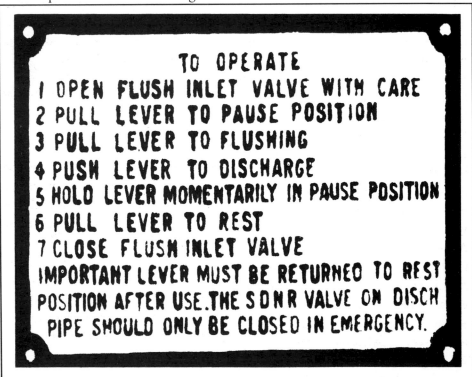

TO OPERATE
1 OPEN FLUSH INLET VALVE WITH CARE
2 PULL LEVER TO PAUSE POSITION
3 PULL LEVER TO FLUSHING
4 PUSH LEVER TO DISCHARGE
5 HOLD LEVER MOMENTARILY IN PAUSE POSITION
6 PULL LEVER TO REST
7 CLOSE FLUSH INLET VALVE
IMPORTANT LEVER MUST BE RETURNED TO REST
POSITION AFTER USE. THE SONR VALVE ON DISCH
PIPE SHOULD ONLY BE CLOSED IN EMERGENCY.

Replica of notice posted in submarine heads

Helping Hand

I was torpedoed in the Atlantic, and the U boat commander told us we'd be picked up within twenty four hours - and we were. They radioed for help, and one of our destroyers came for us. I think that happened quite a lot.

Albert West - Litherland

An Old Salt

At the start of the war I was serving my apprenticeship as a marine engineer, for Elders, and when war broke out they put all the lads to sea as junior engineers. I sailed with them for two years, and the last job I was on was the *"Macon"*. She was torpedoed, two days out of the Azores, and I was in a lifeboat for ten days. We lost two men from the lifeboat, one went over the side and the Chief Engineer died in front of us. You can't describe it.

When we were picked up, by the *"Londonderry"*, we were covered in salt water boils, and they put us in a bath to wash all the salt water off, and it seemed ironic that only an hour before we were fighting over an inch of water.

Anyway I decided that was enough for me, if I'm going to sea, I'm going in a ship I can fight with, so I joined the Royal Navy. There was quite a few served in both, the Merchant had its own brand - what you call T124X, they were merchant men under naval discipline. I came unstuck, because being familiar with docks and ships and so on, they put me in the special service unit, I ended up in the Royal Naval Commando Unit. You used to go in before the landings, and try to secure the docks, I was in North Africa, went in about six hours before in darkness, so I ended up in an even more dangerous position!

Jack Murphy-Runcorn

Avoiding the enemy

One of the vessels I served on was a concrete ship, most unusual, the hull was four and a half inches thick, the *"Lady Walmer"*. She was built for the navy and the idea was to avoid magnetic mines.

I was on leave during the May blitz . and when the ammunition ship blew, you could feel the blast blowing against your trousers five miles away..

Thomas Frederick Edwards- Wallasey

Makeshift nurses

There were 14 gunners on board and 12 of them went down with malaria, so the two of us who weren't ill had to do four hours on, four hours off 'til we got back to England.

On the four off, you had to look after the invalids. They were all in one dormitory, port holes were closed because we were low in the water, and the smell - my God, it was horrible... sympathy wore a bit thin.

Jimmy Passey-Huyton

Lady in White

The "Lady in White", in Durban, used to come down and sing to all the troop ships, "Land of Hope and Glory". And then all the people would come and take you out for the day. This was in the war, they really appreciated you.

Arthur Burch-Woolton

Wish me luck...

I was on the "*Duchess of Bedford*" for two or three runs, mostly taking evacuees to Canada, mainly children. While I was on that ship, we took Gracie Fields and Monty Banks out.
I waited on her, she had the main cabin, the bridal suite they called it.
She was very friendly. When we got to Halifax, we were embarking a lot of Canadian soldiers to come over to Britain and she sang. It was fabulous. She sang through loudhailers as the soldiers were coming on board...Of course she sang "Wish me Luck as you Wave Me Goodbye".

Frank Walker-Wallasey

Just Another day

I was on the last convoy, halfway across the Atlantic, on the "*Ocean Glory*" when they announced VE Day. We just took it as another day, no celebration or anything.

Jim France-Runcorn

Painting for peace

We were in Sydney on VJ day and there were four more "Blueys" alongside the circle of quays, I was on the "*Nesta*", she had the tallest funnel in the world at that time, 98 ft. and the orders came from the shipping office to paint the funnel in peacetime colours. Well, normally it was a job and finish, straight for your drink or whatever. But we were still coming down two days later, all the others had finished.

Arthur Burch-Woolton

Prize of war...and piracy

My first ship was a troop ship, the "*Empress of Australia*" which used to be the Kaiser's yacht...I cant remember her original name...I joined her about 1951...after the war she'd been taken as a war prize by the British government...but she'd been sabotaged, so if you went into a bathroom, fuel oil came out of the taps.
It cost a lot to refurbish.
I went to Alfred Holts then, a lovely family company.
We were sailing to Singapore and Hong Kong, and there was a lot of piracy going on there then, there still is. Last year, nine pirates were hanged in the Far East.
We went to one of the Indonesian Islands, and the captain issued us with a letter, warning us. We used to have to go on watch with a pick axe handle, but the Japanese were much more severe. I remember we were on deck

```
                              m.v. "BELLEROPHON". Voyage 19/H.
                              - - - - - - - - - - - - - - - -

        - W A R N I N G   T O   C R E W   &   P A S S E N G E R S -

                    - THIEVING   AT   BELAWAN -

   ALL MEMBERS OF THE CREW AND PASSENGERS ARE WARNED THAT THIEVING IS RIFE

   AT BELAWAN. DO NOT LEAVE YOUR ROOM VACANT EVEN FOR A MOMENT WITHOUT SHUTTING

   AND SECURING PORTS OR WINDOWS AND LOCKING THE DOORS. IN ADDITION DO NOT LEAVE

   FOUNTAIN PENS, CIGARETTE LIGHTERS ETC, IN OPEN VIEW IN THE ROOM.

      ONLY ONE DOOR GIVING ACCESS TO ACCOMMODATION WILL BE LEFT OPEN. ALL OTHERS

   WILL BE LOCKED AND BOLTED. THE HEAD OF EACH DEPARTMENT WILL MAKE ARRANGEMENTS

   FOR ONE OF THE DEPARTMENT TO KEEP A CONSTANT WATCH AROUND THEIR ROOMS.

      SMALL ARTICLES OF VALUE, WATCHES, JEWELRY, OR MONEY WILL BE LOCKED IN THE

   MASTER'S SAFE, IF HANDED IN, IN A SEALED PACKET WITH OWNER'S NAME.

      YOU ARE ADVISED TO LOCK YOUR DOOR AT NIGHT WHEN ASLEEP IN YOUR ROOM, WHILE

   IN PORT.




                       Sgd..........................Master.
```

Crew warning, M.V *"Bellerophon"*

at six o'clock one morning and there was some sort of ceremony going on on a vessel across the dock, and apparently they were chopping some guy's hand off, someone they'd caught, and they were allowed to do it, apparently, the Indonesian Government didn't stop them.

It was all very clinical, a doctor there, but you could hear the screams, it was terrible. They used like a ceremonial sword, they just wapped the guy's hand off.

Bruce Ferguson-Runcorn

41

Cartoon of the very small Frank 'Winkle' Walker on Parade inside POW camp.

Chapter Three: All Ashore

I gave up my days of want and need,
And sailed with White Star, Cunard and P&O
On the *"Britannic"*, the *"Mary"* and *"Arcadia"*,
Far away and long ago.'

There are still many Merseysiders who recall the days of the great liners, crowds at the landing stage waving and cheering, brass bands playing. Many local men and women worked on those floating palaces, waiting on First, Second and Tourist class passengers. Cruising is back on the Mersey, but the romance of the thirties, forties and fifties has gone forever.

Luncheon card menu for 'The Dominion' Dining Car service aboard the Canadian Pacific Railway service. These trains linked up with the CPR ships to take passengers arriving from Europe across North America.

"The Dominion"

Luncheon Selections

(Price opposite each Entree includes Fruit Juice or Soup, Vegetable, Potatoes, Dessert and Beverage)

Tomato Juice   Grapefruit Juice
Old-Fashioned Navy Bean Soup   Hot or Jellied Consomme

Boiled Fresh Beef, Horse-Radish Sauce......................2.70
Fricassee of Chicken with Vegetables, en Casserole............2.60
Fried or Grilled Fresh Fish, Lemon Wedges 2.30
Salmon and Sliced Egg Salad or Spring Vegetable Combination Salad......1.80
(Vegetables not served with Salad Meals)

Parsleyed Boiled Potatoes   Whipped Potatoes
Buttered New Cabbage   Garden Green Peas

Ice Cream with Wafers   Fresh Rhubarb Pie
                Date-Tapioca Pudding, Lemon Sauce
           Canadian Cheddar or Swiss Gruyere Cheese and Biscuits

Assorted Bread   Rolls, Hot or Cold
        *Coffee   *Tea   Milk
                        *Iced if desired

SPECIAL LUNCHEON
1.60
Hot Chicken Sandwich with Cream Gravy
Garden Green Peas
Ice Cream with Wafers
Coffee   Tea   Milk

It is with pleasure and pride that we call attention to the desire and willing-
ness of all our employees to give their utmost in service and special attention
and they, as well as ourselves, would appreciate your criticisms as well as your
commendations.

J. L. Sugden, Manager, Sleeping, Dining and Parlor Cars, Montreal

Help Yourselves

I did the maiden voyage on the "*Mauretania*" in June 1939. She was magnificent. I got the best job on the ship, saloon deck man - you always got the tips there.

When we got to New York, the passengers went ashore, and all the aristocrats and scroungers came on board for cocktail parties every night...but they were not served.

The law in New York then was that stewards could not serve in port, so they helped themselves to drinks - that's the way it was then.

Mick Sheehan-Canada

The new RMS *Mauretania*

Once a Cunard man, always a Cunard man.

After the war, the "*Mauretania*" was refitted as a passenger ship, and I was an officer steward, and then a first class waiter, going to New York.

It was very nice, first class passengers dressed for dinner. It became first, cabin and tourist, because they did away with third class then...but they never mixed. They had masters of arms on the ships to keep passengers in their own areas.

Lots of famous people sailed on the Cunard vessels in those days, I had the privilege of serving Lana Turner, who was on her honeymoon, Herbert Morrison, and Sir Thomas Beecham, and many more.

We used to buy stores in the various

ports and bring stuff home, canned stuff, butter, I even used to bring joints home and put them in the butchers shop at the bottom on the road, because everything was rationed here then.

One chap I knew, he was a waiter, he worked in New York before the war on the railroad, putting the sleepers down, and he was what we called a "gandy dancer", anyway he was a Liverpool Yank because he talked with an American accent. He'd jumped ship to work in America and then came back.

I used to go to J. Bonds on Broadway for my suits, trilby hats, and "Fruit of the Loom" underwear. We had cherries and strawberries on our under-keks then, long before it was fashion.

You always got good tips off the Americans, but you could be serving the first class passengers and something might go wrong, and you'd be sent to third class - you only got what we called " hot half crowns" there. It was the least you could bloody well get for a tip!

Andrew Lockett-Maghull

Lipstick and nylons

I was in New York for VE Day, ticker tape and all that, I used to buy make up for my mum, and nylons. If you went around Woolworths there you could get anything you wanted.

And of course you could get all the records with the top American stars as well. You could get jeans as well then,

Decorative map of the North Atlantic by William McDowell. -Cabin Foyer-A Deck, *Mauretania*

Cabin Lounge RMS *Mauretania*

they weren't out here. You used to go to the Chinese laundries in New York and you could buy a shirt for a dollar, those that hadn't been claimed, but you took pot luck because sometimes they'd have only one sleeve, or the tail would be ripped.

Our uniform was a pair of blue trousers and a white jacket done up tight to the neck like a mandarin collar …and the buttons would be of the particular shipping company.

On Cunard, uniform for breakfast and lunch was a tuxedo, a waistcoat and a black straight tie, but for dinner, you had to change into a stiff white fronted shirt, wing collar, blue tie and white waistcoat.

Norman Broadbent-Childwall

Them and us

I was a bell boy with C.P.R. My first ship was the "*Duchess of Richmond*". That was a four and a half month cruise just before the war.

I did messages and all the running around for the passengers. They'd ring their bell and I would see what they wanted…what struck me most was the disparity between rich and poor.

There were eight bell boys in one room…we wore a pill box hat, like a waistcoat jacket with nineteen brass buttons.

No shirt underneath, it was buttoned right up.

Frank Walker-Wallasey

SPANS THE WORLD

Vodka and Caviar

I ended up as Maitre d' of the Queen's Grill in *QEII*. You wear all white, and you are totally responsible for the running of the restaurant. In those days, you never saw people for breakfast, they'd appear for cocktails at noon, on deck.

I served many famous people during my time, Jimmy Saville, Rod Steward, Natalie Wood, Robert Wagner, I served them all as a waiter over the years. But my favourite all the years I was on the QEII was a couple from Texas, General and Mrs. Hirsch. They were lovely people, but unfortunately all she lived on was caviar and vodka.

I remember her coming down one morning, for coffee, and she asked me to look after a plastic bag. I shoved it in the back of the dumb waiter, behind the coffee cups, and thought no more about it.

Next thing was, the Maitre d' at the time - who we all called "The Lord" - came up with two security officers and said that Mrs. Hirsch had lost over a million dollars' worth of jewellery. I said I'd seen her wearing her emeralds the night before, but that was all. I'd forgotten about the plastic bag - and of course, when I remembered, I retrieved it, and all the jewellery fell out.

He died a few years later on a world cruise, and I believe she fell over the side of her yacht and drowned.

Norman Broadbent-Childwall

Norman Broadbent, Maitre d'- QE II

Liverpool Yanks

There were three Empress boats, we always sailed at 4.30pm on Friday, and there used to be hundreds on the quayside, it was very emotional.

I was on the same run 'til 1957 - Liverpool-Greenock-Quebec-Montreal, and in the winter we sailed from Liverpool to New York and then the West Indies.

The real "Liverpool Yanks" were the ones who worked on the "*Queen of Bermuda*" and the "*Ocean Monarch*". In those days, if they went out to New York, they had to stay there for two years, for tax purposes. And all they were doing was a six day trip to Bermuda, from New York.

They made a lot of money, no tax, and they were able to buy everything we couldn't - we were the poor boys.

I eventually became a second bar keeper on the "*Empress of France*" and one thing you always did when you came back to Liverpool, you had a food parcel made up of meat, tins of fruit, tins of salmon, all the luxuries you couldn't get at home.

The clothes we bought in New York and Montreal were a quarter of the price at home, and they made people's eyes turn. I used to have a rented car waiting for me when I docked in Gladstone, and I'd use that until sailing day...that's why they called us what they did.

I used to have a pink suit, with elegant, thin trousers, no one had ever seen the like...

There was always friction between Cunard and Canadian Pacific, they thought they were better than us because of the "*Queen Mary*".

We were taking first class passengers, as well as five hundred emigrants on the £10 assisted passage, from 1952-60. You could always tell the ones who would be coming back. There were a lot of women on their own, most of them did not come back, nurses and service people.

In 1956, there was the Hungarian revolution, and C.P. took literally all the Hungarian refugees, they had travelled by train across the continent to Liverpool, and then to Canada. We did three or four trips...It was a good thing for us because the Government gave us a guaranteed tip, so if you were looking after a woman, and her children, you could be making £50 in tips, good money in those days, just for waiting on.

It was a sad time for them. You'd see a lady with six or eight children, and you'd be helping to feed them, they'd lost everything. None of those came back.

We all realised it was on the dwindle, because the airlines were coming in, the emmigrants had gone because Canada had pulled the plug, and there was friction between the Liverpool boys and Southampton, they were called "the mushies"... of course, it was cheaper to sail from there.

Roy Chambers - Llandudno

Garlic Days

I also sailed with C.P.R., on the "*Empress of France*" and the "*Canada*". When she burned out in Gladstone Dock, I was at home, on leave. She was just lying on her side there... It was sad.

But they'd had so many advance bookings that the company bought a French ship called the "*De Graas*". We had to go on board in France and bring her back to Liverpool, and the smell of garlic throughout that ship - it was unbelievable...horrible...and all the signs were in German, because it had been German owned before that.

They did a quick paint job on her, white with the red and yellow squares on the funnel for C.P.R. and we sailed to Montreal.

It was a horrible ship, you had to walk up and down fourteen stairs to the restaurant, with loaded trays.

There wasn't much difference between Cunard and C.P.R., they both worked you bloody hard. Up at six, do a bar stock, carry crates of beer and drinks to various bars...get your bucket and kneeler from under your bunk, do a scrub out of various areas...it was nearly all lino in those days. Then into the restaurant to get ready for breakfast. You'd never lay up the night before in case of bad weather, you might lose all the dishes.

After breakfast you had what they called a "side job", vacuuming or washing glasses, or silver, or you might have the job of cleaning the port holes. ...next, serve lunch. You'd have to eat "on the wing". Then help serve afternoon teas, and then wash up.

You'd get about an hour in your cabin, then back up to serve dinner. It was hard, but I loved it.

Norman Broadbent-Childwall

Ship's lists

About two weeks before sailing, a list of names would be sent in from Cunard Building. This would be updated and about three days before sailing what was known as the "steward's list" and was printed on a large sheet of paper. Then the day before sailing, final names were added and this list - the Purser's list - and was printed .

A few copies, on our airmail paper, were sent to New York, for FBI and Immigration Authorities to check for "undesirables".

The final passengers book was then made up. First class had to have a minimum of sixteen pages...the cover would be on parchment paper, with the Cunard logo and a picture of the particular ship. Names were in strict alphabetical order, and males before females in families.

This book had to be on the bed in the cabins two hours before passengers embarked.

Ken Blasbery-Runcorn

Good news, bad news

We published a daily paper on board, the wireless operator would receive all the details and then the paper was printed. I remember receiving news of the outbreak of war, heading for Vancouver, and we heard about the end of the war in mid Atlantic.

Thomas Frederick Edwards- Wallasey

End of Empire

I was fascinated by the Bibby boats, their names all ended with "shire".
They were bringing families and troops back from India and different places, after independence and so on, and they

always had the military band of that battalion on the landing stage, and they used to march up and down the stage and play, and it was a wonderful sight. That was the end of an era, that, the end of the Empire. It wasn't long after that the liners disappeared.

Alan Richards-Ledsham

Arriving in style

I joined the "*Caronia*", the Green Goddess they called her, Cunard of course, that would be about 1948.

We came down to Liverpool on her trials, the Duke of Edinburgh was on her. It was on the Pathe newsreel, as

The 'shires'

The Bibby Line introduced short cruises in the 30s, sailing to the Mediterranean, and by 1936 were running a service to Palma, which had then become a popular tourist attraction.

Later, transportation and repatriation of troops kept several of their ships busy, as well as emigrants to Australia.

At one time, they had six ships carrying troops including the "*Lancashire*" 'til 1956, and the "*Cheshire*" a year later. But in the 1960s, when the jumbo jet started carrying larger numbers of passengers, the ocean going passenger trade fell away.

Christina Spencer-Mossley Hill

she came into Gladstone dock, simply because she was the largest liner built since the war. The largest funnel, too. She was a beautiful ship.

She never carried cargo, you know, not like the others did...just cruising, luxury rooms, all Americans on board.

We went into New York with a line of tugs each side, and as we entered Pier 90, the place was full of people.

Everyone knew you were a seaman, you dressed well, they'd know where you'd been by your tie, and your suits, we bought them in Sachs, in New York.

Bill Sheridan-Netherton

Sunny Holiday Cruises to the Mediterranean

GIBRALTAR, MARSEILLES, EGYPT
GIBRALTAR and TANGIER, for SOUTHERN SPAIN and MYSTERIOUS MOROCCO.

Return Fare from Liverpool returning to Plymouth or London ... **£16**

Available Outwards from S.S. "Yorkshire," 16th March, to S.S. "Yorkshire," 28th September, 1934, inclusive, to return Homewards up to and including S.S. "Yorkshire," 1st December from Marseilles, and 3rd December from Gibraltar.

Passengers holding Return Tickets to Gibraltar have the option of returning by Steamer of the P. & O., Henderson, Orient, Union Castle, or Rotterdam Lloyd Lines, subject to any adjustment of fares and provided accommodation is available.

MARSEILLES, for ROMAN FRANCE and THE RIVIERA.

Return Fare from Liverpool returning to Plymouth or London ... **£20**

Available Outwards from S.S. "Yorkshire," 16th March, to S.S. "Yorkshire," 28th September, 1934, inclusive, to return Homewards up to and including S.S. "Yorkshire," 1st December from Marseilles, and 3rd December from Gibraltar.

Passengers holding Return Tickets to Marseilles can return from that Port by P. & O., British India, Blue Funnel, Henderson, Union Castle, or Rotterdam Lloyd Lines ; from Toulon or Naples by Orient Line, or from Genoa via Algiers to Southampton by Nederland Line, subject to any adjustment of fares and provided accommodation is available.

Passengers to Marseilles have also the option of returning overland first-class by rail via Paris to London.

EGYPT. Liverpool/Port Said returning to Plymouth or London, **£35**

Available Outwards from M.V. "Worcestershire," 25th May, to M.V. "Cheshire," 14th September, inclusive, to return Homewards up to and including S.S. "Yorkshire," 26th November from Port Said.

OUTWARD SAILINGS.

VESSEL.	Leave Liverpool.	Arrive Gibraltar.	Arrive Marseilles.	Arrive Port Said.
S.S. "Yorkshire" ...	16th March	21st March	23rd March	29th March
M.V. "Shropshire" ...	29th March	3rd April	5th April	11th April
S.S. "Oxfordshire" ...	13th April	18th April	20th April	26th April
M.V. "Staffordshire" ...	27th April	2nd May	4th May	10th May
S.S. "Gloucestershire" ...	11th May	16th May	18th May	24th May
M.V. "Worcestershire" ...	25th May	30th May	1st June	7th June
M.V. "Cheshire" ...	8th June	13th June	15th June	21st June
S.S. "Yorkshire" ...	22nd June	27th June	29th June	5th July
M.V. "Shropshire" ...	6th July	11th July	13th July	19th July
S.S. "Oxfordshire" ...	20th July	25th July	27th July	2nd August
M.V. "Staffordshire" ...	3rd August	8th August	10th August	16th August
S.S. "Gloucestershire" ...	17th August	22nd August	24th August	30th August
M.V. "Worcestershire" ...	31st August	5th Sept.	7th Sept.	13th Sept.
M.V. "Cheshire" ...	14th Sept.	19th Sept.	21st Sept.	27th Sept.
S.S. "Yorkshire" ...	28th Sept.	3rd Oct.	5th Oct.	11th Oct.

HOMEWARD SAILINGS.

VESSEL.	Leave Port Said.	Arrive Marseilles.	Arrive Gibraltar.	Arrive Plymouth.	Arrive London.
M.V. "Staffordshire" ...	18th March	23rd March	25th March	29th March	30th March
S.S. "Gloucestershire" ...	1st April	6th April	8th April	12th April	13th April
M.V. "Worcestershire" ...	15th April	20th April	22nd April	26th April	27th April
M.V. "Cheshire" ...	29th April	4th May	6th May	10th May	11th May
S.S. "Yorkshire" ...	13th May	18th May	20th May	24th May	25th May
M.V. "Shropshire" ...	28th May	2nd June	4th June	8th June	9th June
S.S. "Oxfordshire" ...	13th June	18th June	20th June	24th June	25th June
M.V. "Staffordshire" ...	27th June	2nd July	4th July	8th July	9th July
S.S. "Gloucestershire" ...	11th July	16th July	18th July	22nd July	23rd July
M.V. "Worcestershire" ...	25th July	30th July	1st August	5th August	6th August
M.V. "Cheshire" ...	8th August	13th August	15th August	19th August	20th August
S.S. "Yorkshire" ...	22nd August	27th August	29th August	2nd Sept.	3rd Sept.
M.V. "Shropshire" ...	5th Sept.	10th Sept.	12th Sept.	16th Sept.	17th Sept.
S.S. "Oxfordshire" ...	18th Sept.	23rd Sept.	25th Sept.	29th Sept.	30th Sept.
M.V. "Staffordshire" ...	1st Oct.	6th Oct.	8th Oct.	12th Oct.	13th Oct.

For particulars apply to :

or BIBBY BROS. & CO., Martins Bank Building, Water Street, LIVERPOOL. 22, Pall Mall, LONDON. S.W ..

Previous page:
Bibby Line Holiday
Cruise Brochures.

Left:
Typical prices and
timetables for Bibby
Line Holiday Cruises
from Liverpool.

Below:
The Bibby cargo liner
SS *Oxfordshire*. Built
in 1912 she served as a
Hospital Ship in both
World Wars.

51

Green Goddess

My first Cunard ship was the "*Media*", they carried 250 passengers, they used to say along the docks.. "Those ships submerge once you get to the Bar, and come up in New York", because they used to roll like mad.

I was on the "Green Goddess" for ten years - the "*Caronia*" - they called her that because she was painted three different shades of green, to keep her cool in the tropics.

I remember one particular character on the "*Caronia*", a Miss McBeth ... she outlived three of her companions whilst I was on board. She never left the ship, the only time she went home was when we went into dry dock. She had the same stateroom, she literally lived on board.

She did every world cruise. She used to recognise you by your feet, because she couldn't lift her head up and during the later years on the "*Caronia*", the waiter who looked after her had to puree her food, like baby food, and her companion would feed her.

I heard that she was worth millions ...she owned the Bethlehem Steel Company in the States.

Norman Broadbent-Childwall

Facing page: A typical Cunard programme

Below:
The programme of events and entertainments for RMS *Franconia, 1953.*

THE CUNARD STEAM-SHIP COMPANY LIMITED
R.M.S. " FRANCONIA ·

PROGRAMME OF EVENTS
[Subject to alteration]

TOURIST CLASS

Thursday, June 11, 1953

9-00 a.m.	Deck Games available	Sports Deck
10-15 a.m.	Cinema	Cinema
	" The Ringer "	
	Presenting : Herbert Lom, Donald Wolfit, Mai Zetterling, Greta Gynt and William Hertnell	
11-00 a.m.	Mid-Morning Music (Relayed)	Public Rooms
2-00 p.m.	Cinema (Repeat)	Cinema
4-00 p.m	Relayed Tea Music	Public Rooms
9-15 p.m.	Cinema (Repeat)	Cinema
9 30 p.m.	Keno (Bingo, Housie-Housie)	Smoke Room
10-30 p.m	Dancing to Recorded Rhythm	U. Prom. Dk. Lounge

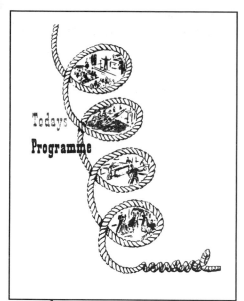

A welcome to Her Majesty

I was in charge of the "*Gothic*" - a Shaw Saville ship, when she was being prepared for the royal tour, this would be 1953/4. The refurbishment was done in Cammell Lairds. She'd been a passenger ship which carried eighty first class passengers, plus cargo. They brought the furniture from Buckingham Palace.

They had to put all sorts of special equipment on board, six radio stations for instance, it was so powerful that if they were going to use more than one of those at a time, you'd get sparks and electric shocks from the rigging, so they blew a whistle, and everyone had to stand away.

We had to crawl through the entire ship, checking the security. Imagine that now, just two people to secure a liner that size for the Queen.

Harry Hignett- Wallasey

Yo Ho Ho.. and a bottle of rum

The "*Queen Mary*" was my favourite ship, there'll never be another, she had style and there was something about her, as soon as you got on board, there was an aura.

I had breakfast on the "*Queen Mary*", with champagne, and because they knew I liked the cherries, they gave me a big tumbler full. I'd been up all night, because I was on a very good table..

I remember being on one of the Caribbean ships, and the air conditioning broke down, so we took all the passengers to the rum factory on Bacardi Island, and got them drunk.. They all had to be carried back in relays, and in the meantime we'd fixed the air conditioning. I reckon here'd have been a mutiny otherwise, but that's some years ago that.

Jenny Kemp- Waterloo

It wasn't done

We had four female staff, a hairdresser, chief stewardess, second stewardess and a nursery stewardess. They had their own sitting room, we'd occasionally meet on deck, but we never socialised...it wasn't done.

We never socialised with the crew, except when it was an Indian national day, we as ship's officers would be invited to have a meal with them. When I started at sea, even the engineers never called each other by their Christian names.

David Eccles- Aigburth

Silver Screen and Strict Tempo

I used to look after the Empress Room, and you had to get down on your knees and scrub the floor, the size of a ballroom, and then you'd polish it...and that was all part of your duty. In the afternoon, you'd put a sheet on the floor and it became a cinema.

Roy Chambers-Llandudno

Blue steel

I was about three years on the "*Australia*". I went to the breaker's yard with her. Every one of the Empress liners had what they called the Empress Room, and it was like a ballroom. The "*Australia*" had an open marble fireplace, Italian marble, and an oil painting, and that was presented to Captain Bell for getting the ship to the breaker's yard for her last trip.

She was bought by the British Iron and Steel Corporation and because she was made of blue steel, we were told she was going to be made into Blue Gillete razor blades.

I went on the "*Empress of Scotland*" then, from Liverpool to Quebec and Montreal in the summer months, Bahamas and the States in winter.

Two of the regular passengers were millionaires, you could say they owned London between them, the man they called "King Cotton", Jack Cotton, and Charles Clore. We used to get £7 a month salary then, and he gave me a five pound note for carrying his birthday cake.

We had a chap from Birkenhead, Sammy Bromfield, he used to run the Empress Room on board, and she then had the longest bar afloat, they called it the Rainbow room because of the lighting. At the end of every voyage, Sammy used to put a brand new white jacket on and all these people used to come and sign it...he had a collection of them.

Bruce Ferguson-Runcorn

Previous page The *Empress of Australia*

Right: Bruce Ferguson with 'King Cotton' and birthday cake, on board the *Empress of Scotland*

Can't see the wood.

I was a cabinet maker/joiner, and I went on the "*America*", she was the ship that took the Blue Riband away from Britain.

Having been brought up with timber, I was horrified to find out that the only wood on board - and they were so proud of this - were the four chopping blocks in the galley...all the doors were in pastel shades of plastic.

Colin Sharp-Bromborough

Raise your glass..

The *Empress of France* had the finest Pig and Whistle, the full beam of the ship, and they had panels with murals of the Everton and Liverpool football teams.

Stan Amos-Moreton

Captain of a Queen

I always wanted to go to sea, mainly because it was in the family. My great grandfather, on my mother's side, was Master of one of the Boston tea clippers, and on my father's side, my grandfather was master of a sailing yacht.

In 1950, I went to sea as an apprentice officer with the Cunard White Star, as it was then...she was called the "*Arabia*", a cargo ship. They had a big cargo fleet in those days.

I was indentured to the company, my parents paid £50, and the training was full, everything from painting the top of the mast to scrubbing the bilges...in some ways, you were cheap labour.

From when I joined, to when I became Master, was 32 years. In those days, Cunard's progression was that you didn't join the passenger ship fleet until you got your Master's ticket. Cunard in those days was the epitome of the Merchant Navy - P & O might disagree with me, though!

Cunard's passenger fleet was of course topped by the two Queens, and they had the "*Caronia*", the "*Mauretenia*", "*Franconia*" and of course later the "*Ivirnia*", "*Saxonia*", "*Corinthia*" and "*Sylvania*" - I sailed on all of those bar the "*Ivirnia*".

In those days the relationship between the deck officers and the passengers was very limited. You were not allowed in public rooms. You could sneak into the back row of the cinema, but ironically you ate in the first class restaurant, you had your own table there.

The "*Caronia*" was built specifically for cruising, and that was a totally different way of life to the mail ships. She went on world cruises, and you had a great deal more contact with the passengers than you did on the transatlantic ships.

Robin Woodall-Hoylake

A silver trail

I was in charge of the dining saloon on the " *Bellerophon*". They had all the silver laid out in rotation, and I was given a log book with every item itemised, and the superintendent said "At the end of the voyage I want to see everything back there". At the end of the voyage, everything was there and I got a £25 bonus, in an envelope, which you never got on the big liners.

Robin Woodall, Captain QE II

On the liners, you used to take silverware down on trays to the cabins, and it was a good way down, and a long trek back to the galley, so instead of taking stuff back, they used to put it through the portholes!

I've always maintained that you could get into a diver's suit at the Pier Head, and walk to New York or to Canada, following a trail of silverware!

On the passenger liners, the blokes used to get what they called a "docking box" - the cooks used to look after you, they'd call you their "bloods", whatever that meant.

You paid a cook say, ten bob a trip, and after the meals, you'd tell him what you wanted off the first class menu, and regardless of what it was, it was put aside for you, and we were eating Lobster Thermidor, and God knows what else, the best of everything.

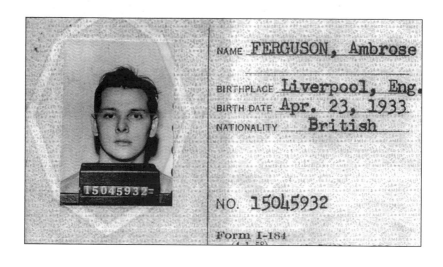

NAME **FERGUSON, Ambrose**

BIRTHPLACE **Liverpool, Eng.**
BIRTH DATE **Apr. 23, 1933**
NATIONALITY **British**

NO. **15045932**

Form I-184

ALIEN CREWMAN LANDING PERMIT
AND
IDENTIFICATION CARD

THE RIGHTFUL HOLDER OF THIS CARD IS AN ALIEN
CREWMAN GRANTED SHORE LEAVE IN THE UNITED
STATES. VALID ONLY IF THE BEARER IS EMPLOYED
ABOARD A VESSEL NOW IN A UNITED STATES PORT.
INVALID FOR ALL PURPOSES 29 DAYS AFTER LAST EN-
TRY TO THE UNITED STATES. THE BEARER IS NOT
PERMITTED TO WORK OR TO RESIDE IN THE UNITED
STATES.

UNITED STATES DEPARTMENT OF JUSTICE
IMMIGRATION AND NATURALIZATION SERVICE

Bruce Ferguson's ID Card. Personal details on front and US Landing
Regulations on rear

I did a trip on an emigrant ship, the "*Tamatora*", the last of the coal burners, run
by Shaw, Saville, to New Zealand...they had separate sections, husbands and
wives were separated for the voyage.

Bruce Ferguson-Runcorn

Travellers' tales

I remember meeting one lady passenger, a very elderly American, who was a survivor of the "*Titanic*"...you see, on Cunard ships, we always had a party for people who had sailed on Cunard before. I was greeting the guests as they came in, and I said to her "Good evening, lovely to see you, when did you sail with us?"

And she said, "On the '*Titanic*'"...and that stopped me short.

She was a child of two and a half then, and I did not have the heart to tell her that the "*Titanic*" was not a Cunarder. But of course, all the survivors were picked up by the Cunard liner "*Carpathia*", so she did have every right to be at that party.

QE II and her crew. 1990

Another passenger sticks in my mind, too...*QEII* carries cars across the North Atlantic, she was like a roll on/roll off ferry ! Not so many now, of course, but I remember one voyage when we had a white Rolls Royce Corniche Convertible on the garage deck. I met the owner, and remarked on his beautiful car. I wondered if he was going to "Do Europe", as Americans did in those days. "No, I'm taking my car back to Rolls Royce to get it fixed, the windscreen wipers don't work".

He drove that car from California to New York, onto *QEII*, off at Southampton, up to Crewe, got his wipers fixed, and two days later he sailed back with us.

Robin Woodall-Hoylake

'We hugged the coasts of Britain
Yet many's the adventure we'd see
Pilots, Coastguards and Tugboat men
All unsung heroes of the sea'

You would be "all at sea" if it were not for the people who provide the essential expertise for seafarers, along our coasts and all over the world.

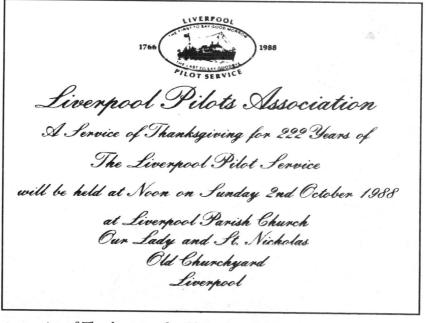

Invitation to service of Thanksgiving for 222 years of the Liverpool Pilot Service

Tugs on the river

When I started there were 57 tugs on the river and the invididual companies had contracts with different shipping lines. The Cock tugs had all Cammell Lairds work, Clan, Harrisons and Bibbys. Alexander's had virtually the monopoly of the liners, CPR, Cunard, all those. Cory's used to do the Blue Funnel boats, and Furnace Withy did the Furnace Lines into Eastham...now there are just two companies, and 11 tugs in the river.

In those days they were all single screw steam tugs, some had open bridges, that was the beginning of the end of steam...they were very primitive. The telegraphs and the wheel were inside what they called the "dodger", and that protected you from the neck down against the elements.

The Captain had fog, wind, rain to cope with, and in those days, his uniform consisted of a sou'wester, oilskin, wellingtons and a towel round his neck for the water running down from sou'wester. It was a difficult job, trying to see where you were going with the sleet and hail in your face.

Alan Richards-Ledsham

Docks and locks

I've been a tugman for forty four years. We used to berth by the ships we were towing for the following day, we'd sleep on board those nights. Of course, that's one of the biggest problems with this river, in other ports you can tie up on jetties, straight out. Here, some ships have only ten or twenty feet clearance going through the locks.

Tug *"Fighting Cock"*-1952. Courtesy of Reflections c/o www.20thcenturyimages.com

"Laying pipelines in Scotland. Tug "Huskisson"

In the old days, there used to be a lock in from the river, and then another one into the dock system, there were two different levels in the docks. It could be a long, long process, up to six hours sometimes.

But they've done away with the interior locks to save on costs and manpower, because each set of gates was manned.

Owen Lawler-Maghull

Trimming the wicks

I applied to all the companies, and got a job with the "Cock" Tugs which was then Liverpool Screw Towing, part of Cammell Lairds. It was a 56 hour week then.

I was 16, and I joined the *"Prairie Cock"* - she was the old Canadian Pacific tug, wonderful boat. It was my duty to scrub the cabins out, polish the lamps, fill and trim the wicks, they were oil lamps then of course, polish the telegraphs, the port holes. No lava-tories, some of them, your first job was to fill the bucket over the side and have it ready. Before that, it was the stoke hole, to be truthful, they had coal on a shovel and three big fires, and that was the life at the beginning. The boats then had coal stoves in the galley, and there were always two black kettles on the go. It was your job to fill them up, make sure there was always boiling water.

Everybody in those days had a tin of "connie-onnie", condensed milk, heating was an old stove with a pipe running up through the deck.

You used to sit on the after deck, and you'd have a "gog" rope coiled in a wooden box, and we had to stay with it in case it had to be slacked up....and there used to be two of us. If it was bad weather, one of us would keep an eye on the skipper waiting for him to shout down, if the wind was in the wrong direction, you couldn't hear him sometimes, so you'd watch for his hand signals.

When the wind was really fierce, and

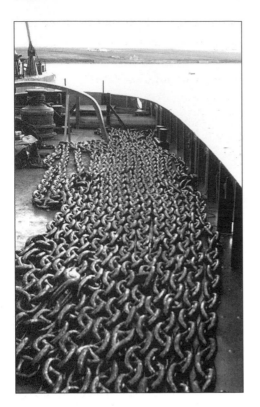

Towing chains on board tug *"Huskisson"*

you were in the middle of a gale, one of my duties was to stand behind the funnel, listening for the pilot's whistle, because there were no radios then, communication was via a pea whistle from the head tug to the pilot and the response was the tug's whistle. It was my job to listen, and if the wind carried the whistle away, you only got half the message. You might shout to the skipper "three" - and sometimes it might have been four, next minute the skipper would blow three on the tug's whistle, and the pilot boat would then blow four times, to make sure you had the right message.

The number of whistles gave different instructions. Three for the north and east, four for the south and west.

Alan Richards-Ledsham

Tricky Bends

I worked on the Ship Canal, on a tug called the *"Ranger"*, a day boat, all manually engineered, you rang down on a telegraph.

It was the heyday, ships up and down the canal all the time. There's a lot of tricky bends, what they call the "birdcage", for instance and very narrow parts where you have to be on your toes. If a ship decided to do what's called "smelling bottom", you'd get a bank of silt on a bend, and you'd have to be prepared to be on the opposite bow ready to pull her into position. It was a very skilled job.

I finished in 1986, there was hardly any work. I miss it like hell, I'd go back today.

Paul Janion-Widnes

Hidden dangers

People just think of tugs in the river, but I got my master's ticket in 1981, and I did ocean towing for about fifteen years, towing all over the world.

I remember towing one of Uglands from Buenos Aires to Hamburg, a nine thousand mile trip, she had been aground, her bottom was ripped out. It was cheaper to repair her there.

We had one job, laying a cable from St. Petersburgh to Denmark. The cable had to be trenched, into the seabed, by the ship we were working with. We ran ahead of this ship, we had to clear any debris, anchors and boulders and stuff that was on the bottom...and this took us through what they call "dumping grounds", areas where all old explosives, gas cannisters, bombs and so on, had been dropped after the two world wars. All countries have these dumping grounds, there are areas in the sea that are designated for that purpose. Some are five or six miles wide in places. They are marked on the charts, so you don't go and anchor there, but you do get the odd trawler that will go through and scatter these things.

We trailed a type of anchor that would pick up any loose wires or anything. It had a meter, which told us if we had touched anything, like a fishing line. We had two German scientists on board, who studied the effects of gas, and as soon as we had a "bite", we'd heave it in and these two guys would go out in their white suits and masks, just like the "X Files", and it was their job to clean these, wash them off to make sure they were safe.

It was a dangerous job.

Alan Richards-Ledsham

Nip and Tuck

Our relationship with the pilots is a very close one; they would join the ship at the bar, bring her in, and then we start assisting the vessel into the locks, through the dock, to her berth. We're a bit like sheep dogs, guiding safely, giving a nip and tuck

Alan Richards-Ledsham

The *"Redoubtable"* (Master - Alan Richards) - towing a "jacket" off West Africa

Towing a very large platform.

Tragedy

In l939, my father was a pilot. He went out - it was a Saturday - and the first thing we knew, my aunt rang us (she was a telephonist with the Dock Company) and she asked my mother if dad had gone out on the Pilot boat, the "*Charles Livingstone*", because there was a boat on the shore. That was the first my mother heard.

What happened at the beginning of the war the lights on the buoys and a lot of the navigation aids were cut out, so theoretically the Germans couldn't find the place. But it was raining, blowing hard, she'd gone out to board ships. Visibility was bad, they were steaming end on and she lost the Bar, couldn't find it, and when the skipper came on the bridge he steered a lot of strange courses, to find it, but he didn't, and eventually they ran ashore. And this, I cannot understand, he believed he was on Rhyl Flats. He sent out a distress call to that effect, lifeboats to go there, but she was off Ainsdale...so there was a terrible waste of time. The boat was lost by being overwhelmed. The weather got worse, my father and a lot of other pilots were sheltering in the lee of the wheelhouse. The sea came up and washed the wheelhouse over the side, and he went with it, as did a lot of others. Some were saved by being in the rigging, one or two actually managed to swim ashore, but there was considerable loss of life.

Three apprentices got awards for bravery. When I joined the service, no one wanted to talk about it.

John Tebay-West Kirby

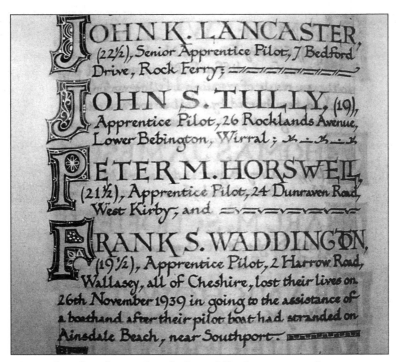

JOHN K. LANCASTER, (22½), Senior Apprentice Pilot, 7 Bedford Drive, Rock Ferry; ⸗⸗⸗⸗⸗

JOHN S. TULLY, (19), Apprentice Pilot, 26 Rocklands Avenue, Lower Bebington, Wirral; ⸗⸗⸗⸗

PETER M. HORSWELL, (21½), Apprentice Pilot, 24 Dunraven Road, West Kirby; and ⸗⸗⸗⸗

FRANK S. WADDINGTON, (19½), Apprentice Pilot, 2 Harrow Road, Wallasey, all of Cheshire, lost their lives on 26th November 1939 in going to the assistance of a boathand after their pilot boat had stranded on Ainsdale Beach, near Southport.

Memorial to those lost on the pilot boat *"Charles Livingstone"*

The last of the station keeping pilot vessels, and one of the first fast pilot launches, which replaced both the station vessel itself and the pilot cutters she carried.

Precision sailing

I was a pilot on the Manchester Ship Canal. You think of a pencil going into a cigar tube, and you realise how precise you have to be.

When I first started, there was very little VHF radio, they usually just gave you what they called a "sky hook" - stay there - so the ship had to stop in the water, and stay in the same position.

Harry Hignett-Wallasey

A bit of "green eye"

I joined the Pilot Service in 1946. You start off as part of the crew, right at the very bottom, everybody's dogsbody.

You'd scrub decks, serve the food - it weeded out a lot of people. It was a left-over regime from the sailing ship days. Most of the passenger ships had company pilots, there was a bit of "green eye" about, because of the prestige.

There are two schools of thought about pilots; they either think you're clad in oilskins and a sou'wester and you grab hold of the wheel, like "Pilot" matches, or you stand, like a gremlin at the Captain's side, saying "watch that bank, mind that buoy".

Generally speaking you stayed in one area, but when we had all the problems with strikes and the fall off in trade, people started to go overseas. In the end, they only needed half the number of pilots we had. In fact the majority of the pilots in Southampton now come from Liverpool.

We have no cutters now, we now have launches, in my time you got aboard a ship and anchored if a berth wasn't ready for you. Most of the entrances we knew have closed now.

John Tebay-West Kirby

Fighting the elements

Probably my most challenging job was being put on board a 200,000 ton tanker , the *"Myrina"*, which broke away from Tranmere Jetty, in January, 1976.

It was the worst gale I've ever experienced - the winds reached over 80 knots, hurricane force, and then down to storm force 10. It was a big tide, nine metres, and near high water you were getting tidal surges of eight feet over the norm...that sank George's stage, and the wind did a lot of damage ashore.

I was put on board by launch, and that was tricky because the ship had actually broken away and she was then ashore on Pluckington Bank.

I had a job getting on because the deck was covered in oil and the crew couldn't carry the ladder across because it was so slippy...and then the battle started.

We had two tugs, she had the port anchor down and started kedging up the river, she went further south and we ended up on Garston Bar, about a thousand feet from the shore. And there she stuck, despite all our efforts. By then another pilot had joined me, a

Shell pilot, and we stayed there all night.

When a tanker discharges, it has what is called an inert blanket over it to stop any explosions...unfortunately, this system had stopped working, so the Captain said he couldn't guarantee the status of the tanks.

We knew she was going to dry out and we didn't know what damage that would do to the hull.

It's a lot of ship sitting on a bank...if pipework or plates split, it could set off a spark.

Eventually we got her off, it was still force 10, and we couldn't get back to Tranmere, so she went out to sea.

John Tebay-West Kirby

"Myrina" off Bromborough

"Myrina" after refloating being towed upwind into deeper water.

A watchful eye

I'm the longest serving at the Radar Station. The first station was established in 1948 but we've moved around a lot over the years.

The job then was nearly all radio, and the men were also telephonists for the main exchange of the Dock Company. They had a telegraph station at Lynas, Anglesey, and I remember they used to have a telegraph machine which had a large roll of paper and the man at Lynas used a morse key to send, and it printed out here. You had to read each individual dot/dash.

We talk to the ships, get information from them, if they have problems we ring the agents, we identify them on radar, mark each one as they come in. We actually organise pilots as well, which we didn't in the past.

Alan Nixon-Wallasey

Guarding our coasts

I was in the Marine Branch of the RAF, where Laurence of Arabia had served. Once I finished there, I joined the Coastguard Service. They said they had a lovely job for me, in Formby, and I said "Where's that?"

It was a portakabin in the sand dunes, sand in the sandwiches, sand in your shorts, sand everywhere!

I did know Liverpool, because being born in North Wales, I was brought here every year to buy my school cap, at Owen Owen, but coming back, I remember saying to my wife "What's all these funny little yellow and red boxes on all the houses?" I honestly didn't know they were alarms.

We were Revenue Men originally, our secondary duty was Search and Rescue, or Saving of Life at Sea as it was then. We do get called "light house men" or "RNLI", people get us confused.

Pilot Apprentices, early 1950s, each holding their 'badge of office'. Left to Right: 'Bosun' with 'rope's end', 'Lampman' with small oil lamp, 'Logman', with official log...to be completed 'in a fair hand', Puntsman- responsible for motor punts, Senior Boathand- acted as Chief Mate ...and 'Junior Lad'- speaks for itself!

Mike Roberts, Coastguard

When I began, we had things like throwing pieces of rope and string around on rockets, rocket rescue gear ...but that's all been disposed of now. Life saving apparatus then was firing rockets out to distressed ships and hauling people ashore by Breeches Buoy, and those rockets were quite lethal...but about 1985, that was all withdrawn.

The reliability now is on helicopters, lifeboats or coastguard rescue teams.

When I joined everything was hand-written, if not in copper plate, then all in log books, now it's computers.

Mike Roberts-Formby

Keeping the river safe

I worked as mate on the floating plant, the "*Salvor*" and the "*Vigilant*", the Dock Board tenders, doing things like buoy changing, surveying, safety duties on the river. The area we covered was more or less from the bar inwards. And when the big tankers started coming in they had guard boats, we were doing that.

I joined in 1967, they had 15 craft then, now it's only three.

They use the crane, the "*Mammoth*", to do the buoys now, with an annual inspection by Trinity House.

The buoys are a lot bigger than you think, the smaller ones - green - they're seven to nine ton, the boat beacon type are around 35 tons, and the central channel markers are 50 tons. We got reports from shipping that lights had been extinguished, for instance, so, weather permitting, we'd go out, change the light. In those days they were all gas buoys, now they're electric, worked from solar panels. The difference is the light on the bar, that works on a flash gun principle, just like a camera flash.

Alan Nixon-Wallasey

Dancing shoes and Christmas trees

My grandfather, Edwin Thomas Abbot, was Master of the Bar Lightship from the 1930s up to the 50s. He'd worked his passage on a clipper ship from Australia. Eventually his son finished up as Master as well, quite a family business. The lightship was on the edge of Liverpool Bay...the "*Alarm*" preceded the boat my grandad was on, the "*Planet*".

There was a miniature lighthouse on the bar light. He was on board when the "*Thetis*" went down.

He used to knit his own socks, and he'd be at sea three weeks out of four. He was what you'd call a Victorian father - my mother loved dancing, and when he came home, he locked her shoes in the sideboard, to keep her in.

When he went back to the "*Planet*", my grandmother unscrewed the back of the sideboard to get at the shoes!

The pilot cutter used to provision the bar light ship, and every Christmas they used to take out a tree, which was nailed to the top of the light.

Michael Molyneux-Wallasey

Edwin Abbot, master of Bar Light Vessel

At the mercy of the seas

I was master of the Mersey Bar Lightship. There were seven crew on her, me, an engineer, a donkeyman - that's the name for a chief fireman, probably after the boilers on the older ships, and four sailors.

The lightship was the "*Planet*" - now in Birkenhead with the historic warships. She was a very nice boat, no engine, no propellor, so if she did break adrift you were at the mercy of the seas. The anchor was made of wrought iron, not cast, it was stronger. There was a spring system on the anchor for bad weather, to absorb the biggest pitching. She had a rudder, and a sail at the after end which we used to keep her into the sea, rather than across it. We had a wave recorder on board, and the biggest I saw when I was on was 27 foot six inches, that's as high as a house.

A lot of people are surprised about the light, there were three foot mirrors, a lens in front, and a 60 watt bulb! That's all it was. The light was on all the time but it rotated...you could see it for 12 miles.

A lot of the AB's used to fish, put the catch in the freezer, and give it to old people's homes when they got ashore.

We did two weeks on, two off. If you were unlucky you got Christmas on board, very unlucky you got New Year as well.

Mersey Missions used to send us out a hamper, no drink, and a tree.

I was on her in September 1972 when she came in...she was towed in, of course, into Waterloo Dock. No special ceremony. They put a LANBY buoy in her place, a Large Automatic Navigational Buoy.

Alan Nixon-Wallasey

Mersey Bar Lightship. The *"Alarm"*

Chapter Five: Trade Winds

In nought but a rusty kettle
We sailed the deepest of the deep
But we had to feed the people back home
Before widows started to weep

Merseyside's seagoing traditions belong firmly with trade; look around you, and you can see many reminders, from grand buildings to renovated docks...of the days when thousands of men sailed from the Mersey around Britain's coast...and around the world.

Tom Taylor and shipmates with local children, Sekondi, West Africa. (Tom on left)

A porridge fight

There was no such thing as the Pool then, so I signed on my next vessel - Harrison's "*Spectator*", just after the first war.
You got one tin of milk for three weeks, one loaf for 24 hours, tea, sugar all weighed out...we were practically starved, you know. We used to get round the cook, there'd be a fight for the porridge pan, scraping it out...we used to pinch spuds, and roast them in the night in the galley.

William Tennant-Bootle

Sailing Ships

I remember the sailing ships. I did a couple of trips on schooners over to Ireland, this would be around l930. We carried coal, brought spuds back.

The accommodation was lousy, you had a stove with coal to heat the place. It was wet and damp. No engines, get out in the Mersey, and tack up the river.

Mick Sheehan-Canada

Dot Dash Dot

I worked for Marconi Marine, and I served in about 30 ships.I couldn't get a job because it was the middle of the slump.
I had never heard of wireless operators, but I decided to join and I went to a radio college in Bold Street. It was night school, learning morse code, telegraphy etc.
Then I got a letter from Marconi and within two weeks I was on my way to Australia, on the "*Orford*".
We signed on for a shilling a month,

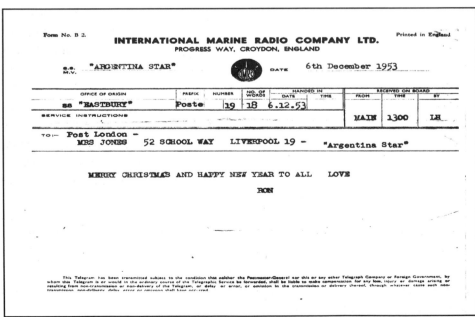

Telegram home to Liverpool from Ron Jones, aboard the *"Argentina Star"* and on facing page, the envelope from Blue Star Line

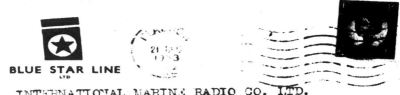

BLUE STAR LINE
LTD

INTERNATIONAL MARINE RADIO CO. LTD.

POSTE RADIO.

MRS JONES
52 School Way
Liverpool 19.

that was a legal requirement to make us members of the crew, but we were always paid by Marconi, never the shipping lines.

The first ship to be fitted with Marconi radio sailed from Liverpool in 1902, she was called the "*Lake Champlain*", and of course, everyone knows the survivors on the "*Titanic*" owed their lives to Jack Phillips, the wireless operator.

It was only short range in those days, but now they've stopped the morse code entirely, and they are talking about closing down coastguard stations...very foolish.

Thomas Frederick Edwards-Wallasey

Lime Juice

In November 1934, I joined a tramp steamer, picking up and dropping cargo all over the world. In some ports you had to do the work of stevedores as well.

I remember a ship called the "*Fife*". I was eighteen months on that one. We took a load of copper ore to Baltimore and then we loaded with scrap for Japan - because they were starting to build up then, armaments, you know. Food was awful, the skipper bought the cheapest. Water was scarce, you only got a gallon a day for everything, s**t, shower and shave - that's a seaman's expression! And after a few days you were on salt tack and biscuits, because the bread went green and the meat was starting to walk...they used to give us lime juice, for scurvy.

It took us 59 days to get to Japan because the ship could only do five or six knots.

Mick Sheehan-Canada

Keeping it clean

When I was 20 years old the company brought out a scheme where they had a ship manned by cadets instead of AB's. The money saved was put into a fund called the "Calcus" fund, and any AB who had seatime in, and wanted to go for a mate's ticket, would be interviewed in India Buildings.

That was some interview that was, in the board room, about eight or nine of them around this table, asking questions. "How often do you get bathed", and things like that.

And when I replied, they said "Only once a week?" and I told them my dad wouldn't let me light the fire for hot water more than that in the summer.

Bill Biddulph-Wallasey

Man overboard

At the end of the war, I joined the Merchant Navy, and worked on tramp ships for Harrison Line, Ellermans, City, PSNC, all out of Liverpool.

One of the ships I joined in Garston was the *"Graigwen"* — I signed on in 1949, and I came back in 1951!

She was a bit bigger than a ferry boat, carrying various cargoes; conditions were a bit rough, the first thing you got was a bucket, for bathing. To get the water, you had to take the bucket outside, then go down below where there was a pump, you did a hundred strokes on the pump, and the bucket would be full. Then you'd take it to the galley, put it under a steampipe, and then you'd get warm water.

I remember the stern light went out, and the Chief Officer asked me to go and fix it... I did, and I was washed

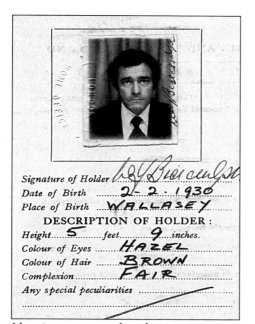

Identity papers and authority to operate a ships radio telephone station — Bill Buddulph.

overboard...and washed back on board by the same wave.

Joseph Williams-Widnes

Broadway Melody

We use to tie up at the bottom of Fourteen Street, in New York, and we went to a place called the Theatre Wing, like a U.S.O. club, but they accepted British Merchant seamen there. You could get a ticket for ten cents, to any Broadway show, or musicals, we used to go to the Paramount and the Roxy, on Broadway, you got a show and the latest movie. I saw Guy Mitchell at the Paramount.

Norman Broadbent-Childwall

Getting your teeth into it

I was on a tramp ship, the *"Hope Range"* sailing out of Newcastle, she was bloody awful. I was an AB on that, I'd left Blue Funnel, because I wanted to see other parts of the world...and the skipper on that had what they called a "skipper's bond", which means he stored the ship personally, and he sold what he bought, at a profit, to the crew.

Food was pretty bad, but we got our own back on him. We found a set of false teeth, put them in his food, and waited for the scream. We were seven months on her, and did two ports. In Korea, he wouldn't give us money to go ashore, and we'd been on board three months. We got no help from the union, they were a joke.

Stan Amos-Moreton

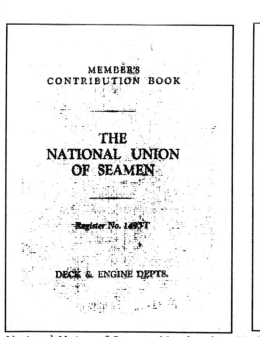

National Union of Seamen Membership Card and list of Union membership benefits paid. 1950. Stan Amos.

Coal burner

My cousin served with Ellermans. He deliberately got himself posted to the last coal burner in the fleet, second mate on the old "*City of Worcester*", and he says it was the only ship on which he served that you looked at the black of your eggs, and not the white, when you went for your breakfast.

Alan McLelland-Mossley Hill

Land's End for orders

I sailed with a Glasgow tramp, the "*Caledonian Monarch*". When you picked up a cargo, you didn't know the actual port you were going to, they used to say "Land's End for Orders", back from the sailing ship times.
What actually happened was you waited for the "Sparks", the wireless operator, to get instructions. We used to head for Europe, say, and during that time the cargo would be sold.

David Eccles-Aigburth

Poor relations

With the American victory ships, the priority was the crew, and the cargo was second. The port holes on US ships were big enough to get out of, they had ice fountains, fridges, clocks, telephones, laundry, all kinds of amenities. When they got here, the British ship owners took everything out.

Stan Amos-Moreton

David Eccles, 4th Engineer, on board SS "*Caledonian Monarch*", Muroran, Japan, 1953 and below on right, on board MV "*City of York*", 1956

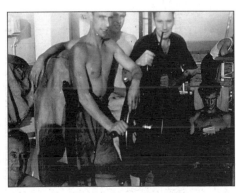 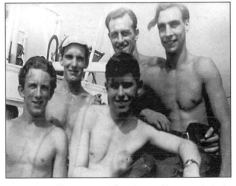

The lads from the MV *'Accra'*… Autumn 1951…where are they now?

Oiling the Wheels

On the "*Nesta*" we took the Australian war brides back. We used to have to oil the prams for them because the salt water seized them up.
And we brought evacuees back from Australia, they went out as children and came back as young ladies and young men.

Arthur Burch-Woolton

A special journey

All the Blue Funnel ships were named from Homer's "*Iliad*". One was called the "*Tindarius*" she was quite old, a coal burner and she was a ship which was used for the Pilgrim route, taking the people to Mecca.
The pilgrims were actually carried in the cargo holds, and we made the three or four tier bunks that they slept in... sadly, we were involved in making the overside chute, which was used for the ones who didn't make it.

Colin Sharp - Bromborough

A yen for sugar

I remember being the first merchant ship into Japan after the war, into Kobe. It was rather interesting, the American troops came on board while we were discharging, and they all had automatic weapons.
We had carried sugar to the Persian Gulf, we were always on the lookout for money, and inevitably a bag would burst. I'd been down in the hold, and brushed all the sugar up. I put it in bags but I'll tell you, it was rather dirty sugar.
In Kobe, with the aid of sign language, you know, I indicated to these Japanese men that I had sugar for sale. So I bought some lady's fans, and a couple of cameras with the money I made. I had to take the money ashore in my shoe because the Americans controlled how much yen you could take into the country.
I made a lot of money because the fans went down well in Cuba.

Brian McEvoy-Wallasey

Getting your own back

I got married in 1950, I was on the "*Apapa*" at the time. You used to get a tablet for malaria each day, and a tot of rum, so all the lads forewent their rum for weeks, and so four or five bottles went into our wedding cake. It had three tiers...it was rationing still then. Anyway, they all came to the wedding so they got their rum back!

Arthur Burch-Wootlon

Body and soul

They had a medical box on board, the principle contents would be condoms, asprin and aluminium paste to deal with certain unmentionable skin complaints – social diseases...and that was your medical care.
Religion – nothing like that. In port there were Missions to Seamen, but there was never a bar there, so they

80

Above: Arthur Burch and wife — and cake
full of rum!.Top right: Arthur and shipmates poolside at Wharf Inn, Apapa.
Right: 'Never mind the payoff, come home sunburned'.
Below: Certificate of Competency as AB. Arthur Burch.1952

Certificate of Competency as A.B.

Nº 016470

MERCHANT SHIPPING ACT, 1948

Granted under the Provisions of the Merchant Shipping (Certificates of Competency as A.B.) Regulations, 1952.

NAME AND DESCRIPTION OF HOLDER

Name in full	Date of Birth	Discharge Book Number (Dis. A)	Height Ft.	ins.
Arthur BURCH	13/3/28	R295313	5	4

Colour of Eyes	Hair	Complexion	Tattoo or other Distinguishing Marks
Hazel	Brown	Fresh	Scar behind r/ear

This is to certify that the above-named has been found duly qualified in accordance with the above-mentioned Regulations, to be engaged in the rating of A.B. in any British Ship registered in the United Kingdom.

Dated this 11ᵀᴴ day of September 19 52

Issuing Officer Dennis McGrath   P. Faulkner   An Under-Secretary of the Ministry of Transport.

Office Date Stamp }

Signature of Seaman A. Burch

E44182 Wt.43375-4170 25M(4) 3/52 Gp.58 F. & C. Ltd. London

weren't terribly popular. They used to have magazines 12 years out of date and chairs around the wall, like a doctor's waiting room.

Brian McEvoy-Wallasey

Playing Safe

When you were on board, they gave you what they called Dreadnoughts, you know, condoms with some ointment for venereal disease..

Arthur Burch-Woolton

Lucrative changing

When our kiddie came along, you had to have coupons for nappies, so I went ashore in America and asked for napkins – diapers they called them. They were 25c each, but if you bought towelling, that was only 10 cents a yard.

So I used to buy so many yards, get the sewing machine out, and of course, what the lads used to say to me was nobody's business, sewing nappies.

Anyway, I had the last laugh, by the end of the three and a half years I was away, I was making nappies for most of them, and making money, too.

Peter Johnson -Seaforth

Living on deck

My first trip with Elders, was in August 1951, as fifth engineer sailing from Toxteth Dock to West Africa. They were a good company to work for, good money.

We carried mostly cement, and on top of the cement, we'd load cars.

Peter Johnson

Coming back, cocoa beans, palm oil, which you had to keep at the correct temperature, to make sure it didn't set, otherwise you couldn't pump it out.

We used to run in competition with Lever Brothers, they were the Palm Line, but we were in a Conference, there was Elders, John Holt, Palm Line and the rates were fixed, so you all got a piece of the cargo.

Above: *SS Prah*, Elder Dempster Lines, Hamburg, May 1952.

Below: Sea Service certificate for a 'strictly sober' Ronald Vaughan. December 1956

We used to pick up "kroo" boys when we got to the coast, from Freetown, or Monrovia. We'd have a hundred or more, in tents, living on deck, they'd have a rice boiler, and they'd wash and eat there.

They would run the winches, load and unload sapele and mahogany logs.

We'd take about 12 passengers as well, what we used to call "empire builders" – people working for the government, and missionaries.

The Elder Dempster Flag flew everywhere, it was the cross of St. George, with a crown in the middle, which was Royal Mail, and in those days, there were more Elders Flags than Union Jacks.

Ronald Vaughan - West Derby

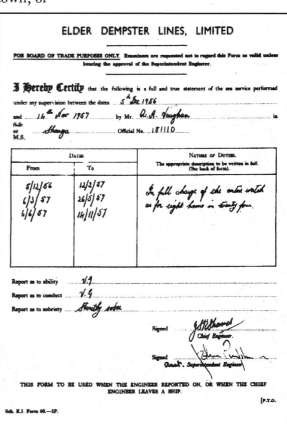

Mal de mer

I suffered with sea sickness all the time I went away, I still had to serve though, I'd do one course and then dive down to the toilets...you still had to work.

Dave Molyneux-Wallasey

Below left: Dave Molyneux and the 'Patroclus' in dry dock- Glasgow 1956.

Below right: Dave Molyneux 'All toffed up'.1959

Overleaf: Shore Leave Pass. Tom Taylor.

Head in the sand

My first trip was down the creeks in West Africa on the "*New Texas*", we carried back palm oil kernels below decks, mahogany, and ostriches, tethered on the upper deck. When they were being moved we used to have to put stockings over their heads, to stop them panicking. I've no idea why they were bringing ostriches back here in wartime.

They didn't give you sheets, it was a straw mattress and two woollen dark blankets, a donkey's breakfast. You were like a teddy bear in the morning, all the blankets had stuck to you.

Thomas Taylor-Warrington

Six Eggs a week

I started my seagoing career with BP, in 1956, the year of the Suez crisis. In those days, BP had 144 ships, the average crew size was about 50, and they were one of the smaller companies. I'd looked at other shipping companies, but some of them struck me as high faluting, Cunard and them, not my cup of tea. Shortly before I started there'd been a lot of changes of rules, about the conditions, food and so on, so from then on, it was government rules rather than shipping companies' pockets. For instance, after the change you had to have six eggs a week...a big improvement.

Alan Nixon-Wallasey

SHORE LEAVE PASS

(A.C.P. Form No. 437)

(GRATIS)

No. 7262/46

الأسم

Name ... T. TAYLOR

الجنسية

Nationality ... BR. Age ... 23

الوظيفة

Function ... A.B.

اسم الباخرة

M. V. MALAYAN PRINOE ... Flag ... BR.

اسم الشركة التابعة لها

Company ... PRINCE LINE

أوراق إثبات الشخصية

Document ... R.242606

LIVERPOOL. 7-12-42

Knowing your place

The Blue Funnel had some peculiar things about it. For instance, the crew got apples and oranges only on Thursday and Sunday; they had cabin tea for the officers, crew tea for the crew. Able seamen got a tin of condensed milk a week, you'd punch two holes in it and then put plugs in to keep the bugs out.

But as a company, they were interested in you. I remember a couple of men were killed and the company put their children through a very high educational system.

Stan Amos-Moreton

Inspection

It was very formal, a hangover from the old days, I think.

The Captain would say "Present my compliments to the Chief Engineer, and ask him, at his convenience, would he take coffee with me". So you'd go and knock on his door, convey that message, and take back the reply: "Thank the Captain, send my compliments, tell him I would be delighted to join him".

And then on a Sunday, at sea, there was always an inspection. You got up at six, and you scrubbed every mortal thing.

If it was stationary, it got washed. If it was moveable, you put it away...and then you scrubbed yourself, and decked yourself out.

At 9.15am, he would start his inspection. Immaculate, white shoes, white socks up to his knees, shorts, crisp, starched shirt...a crease you could shave with...white cap, white gloves.

He would walk around the cabin, run his white fingered glove across the top of the lockers, and if the glove was not spotless, he would say 'S٪.t' and walk out.

And then you'd have to start all over again.

Brian McEvoy-Wallasey

Jack of all trades

I was chief steward, working on container ships and they got rid of a lot of staff so I ended up doing a lot of different jobs, signing people on and off, looking after the medical side and so on.

My medical experience was one week in the A&E at Broadgreen Hospital,

Bryan Wickens on board the "*Torbay*" container ship, 1992

which Blue Funnel organised. I had a white coat on and patients thought I was a doctor, which the staff thought was hilarious.

On board, you had a book and if someone came to you with a rash, you looked at the pictures of rashes in the book to see if they matched...most of the time you were right!

And then there'd be men coming back on board after scraps, eyes hanging out, social diseases as we used to call them, we put them down in the book. We carried a very good dispensary. All the dangerous drugs were in the captain's safe.

I looked after the food, ordered it, and kept the bar stocked. You used to get fresh fruit and vegetables when you were in port, I used to go down onto the dock and barter with locals.

When they reduced the staffing, we lost a lot of engineers, and they put a bleep machine in the engine room so that if it went off, someone would go down and fix it.

I can remember the Chief Engineer saying he'd think more of the bleep machine if it could clean the engine room as well.

Later on, you started getting women on board, cadets and so on, and they'd all come along with their problems, maybe they thought they were safe with me!

Bryan Wickens-Upton

Whiskey Galore

My brother Peter was on a ship called the "*Politician*", and they were shipwrecked off one of the Scottish islands, it ran aground.

He told us about all this whisky they had aboard, and about all the people on the island running to the shore and picking up the bottles and cases of whisky and hiding it.

The crew were put up in locals' houses 'til they went home.

Compton McKenzie later wrote a story called "*Whiskey Galore*", and he changed the name of the "*Politician*" to the "*Cabinet Minister*", but on that island now, they've got a local pub, and they call it the "Polly".

Theresa Bassett-Aigburth

Chapter Six: Women and the Sea

How dutiful the women of Liverpool,
Stewardesses, laundry maids and Wrens,
Who sailed and served, in war and peace,
In those days of undiscovered ends...

For many local women, a connection with the sea was working in the dozens of shipping companies with offices all over town; for others, it was a brief sojourn in the WRNS, doing unglamorous jobs in wartime...and for some, the cruise liners beckoned.

HMS *Wren, 1943*

The Palais Glide

I was 18 years old in June 1935, and I went for a medical examination in Rodney Street, a Dr. Lefanu. He was a formidable character, more used to administering jabs to people bound for West African shores, including what was then known as the Gold Coast. I was starting work at John Holt and Company, who were on the seventh floor of the Royal Liver Building. I worked in the invoicing department, learning about places like Ebute Metta, Fernando Po, Calabar and Koforidua. Cargo included galley pots made of cast iron, sewing machines, bales of cloth and food and drink and of course medical supplies.

The firm owned five ships, all named after members of the Holt family. Two were launched at Cammell Lairds during my time with Holts. They sailed every fortnight, so there was a week of comparative quiet, followed by a frenzied rush as the invoices flooded in. I remember the shipping clerks on their high stools. The seventh floor of the Liver has a wide balcony, with pillars, and one day a girl put a chair outside, to take the sun, amongst the pigeons' nests.

When war was declared, we were given yards and yards of material to make black out curtains for all the windows in the office.

We used to have firm's dances in those days, in the Café Nord in North John Street, an entrancing place with make believe trees, latticed windows and stars on the ceiling and we'd dance the Palais Glide on the top deck of the ferry boat home.

Bettina Thomson-Spital

Dancing with heroes

I was 17 when I lost my brother in the war.

So I hired the Knotty Ash village hall and organised dances and concerts for servicemen. We never charged them an entrance fee. Some of the girls from work - Paton Calverts - provided the entertainment. Ruth Price was a very good pianist and Audrey Symes, Edna Lyons and a few others sang. Irene Widdens was my right hand man.

I managed to obtain extra coupons from the Food Ministry.

The vicar from Knotty Ash increased the charges for the hall, so my dad went to see Father O' Sullivan from St. Aloyisious in Twig Lane, and he let us use his hall on one condition - he would come each time we had a dance to say a prayer. The hall had no drinks licence but Father O' Sullivan overcame that obstacle, don't ask how. From the funds we raised, I'd give the money for bottles of beer, give all the servicemen a ticket and send them, ten at a time, into Father O' Sullivan's office.

We used to collect wounded men from Broadgreen, Whiston and Alder Hey Hospitals, I got permission from the Ministry of Transport for extra fuel.

We also arranged to meet some of the men from Alder Hey in Springfield Park and take them to the Wheatsheaf or the Knotty Ash. They were supposed to be back by a certain time, but of course, nine times out of ten they were late, so we used to help them climb back over the fence.

On one occasion, some sailors came to the Knotty Ash hall, they had heard about the fun we had and enjoyed themselves so much they asked me to write to one of their officers, requesting permission for a party of their mates to have a late pass, to enable them to come to our "do". I received a letter from this officer, thanking me, and inviting some of us girls to a party they were having. We had a wonderful time. But I'm sorry to say that their ship was later torpedoed, with no survivors.

May Fletcher-Tarbock

The black foot gang

I joined the WRNS in 1944, and I was stationed in Tallahewin Castle, which had been condemned by the Americans as being unfit, but they put us in there. The ablutions block was in the middle of the huts, and you had to carry a soaking flannel with you, because by the time you got back to your own hut, you were in what we called the "black foot gang", you had mud all over your feet.

There was a pot bellied stove in the middle of the hut. We all slept in bunks, we scrubbed floors, all of us, whatever your background. In fact one of the girls was a "Lady", and I don't think she'd ever seen a scrubbing brush

Above: Stella Passey - and friend!
Below: Stella Passey in her WRNS days, painted on silk.

in her life, but she had to set to, the same as the rest. Wrens were issued with navy blue knickers and vests. We were given coupons for vests and slippers only, but we'd swap them for a new bra or a pair of shoes. I got the most wonderful greatcoat a sharkskin "Beau Brummel", it fitted me perfectly because I was so small, and I wore it, long after the war.

Eventually I was posted to HMS "*Eaglet*", that was the Liver Building at that time. The Northern Hospital used to be called HMS "*Mersey*". We used to call them HMS "Never Budged", because of course they were buildings, not ships.

I used to go to Derby House every day with signals...they had all the charts with the convoys there and it was horrible to see them taking off ships that had been "bumped".

Stella Passey-Huyton

"Blackouts"

I was a steward at a Fleet Air Arm base in Scotland, looking after the men. We worked in watches, starboard and port...we worked in a white coat, with a blue collar.

The main uniform was black skirt, thick black stockings, black shoes. Our laces all had to be tied the same way. We wore black knickers, we called them "blackouts", and they had elastic in the legs, for when you got in and out of lorries, and a white shirt with stiff starched collar. We wore a front and back stud, just like the men, and when

I got back to civilian life, I still had this red mark around my neck, and the mark of the stud, as well.

Olga Bailey-Fazackerley

Billeted in style

We were quartered in "Tattoy House", 20 Aigburth Drive, it was the Greek Consul's house, and we used to have dances there, because the rooms were enormous. We'd invite sailors, there were a few romances, but not me.

After that, I was in the "slops", the stores, ordering the food, and because I'd been a tailoress, I altered uniforms. This was in Plymouth, and all the shops there had been bombed, so they were set up in great big old houses, with doorways from one department to another.

Joyce Cook-Woolton

In demand

They said I was going to Scapa Flow, and I thought "Hang on, where's that?" On 12 May 1943, I was drafted to HMS '*Proserpine*'...at Lyness in the Orkneys.

I went on what most seamen will remember - the "Jellicoe Express".

Express it never was, it took 24 hours to Thurso. When we arrived at Perth, all female service personel were moved to a separate carriage, which was sealed off from the rest of the train, for the night journey to Thurso. Conditions were reasonable, there was

A WRNS wedding - Joyce Cook

ROLL OF HONOUR
THE AGUILA WRENS

SECOND OFFICER.
Christine Emma Ogle.

THIRD OFFICERS.
Cecelia Mary Blake Forster.
Margaret Eulalie Chappe Hall.
Isabel Mary Milne Holme.
Cecilia Alex Bruce Joy.
Victoria Constance McLaren.
Florence Macpherson.
Kathleen Miller.
Josephine Caldwell Reith.

NURSING SISTER
Kate Ellen Gobbie. QARNS

CHIEF WRENS.
Phyllis Bacon.
Margaret Watmore Barnes.
Cecily Monica Bruce Benjamin.
Dorothy Bonsor.
Madeleine Gladys Cooper.
Mary Grant.
Mildred Georgina Norman.
Elsie Elizabeth Shepherd.
Catherine Johnston Staven.
Beatrix Mabel Smith.
Ellen Jessie Waters.
Rosalie Wells.

Roll of Honour for WRNS lost in war.

a NAAFI like store where we could buy toiletries and so on, there was a clothing store as well, but I always sent my shirt collars home to Liverpol, to be cleaned and starched in a local Chinese laundry.

I was posted to the mail office, dealing with all incoming and outgoing mail for the offices and all shore based sailors. There were 200 Wrens there, and 30,000 fellows! They used to send all the stars up to Scapa. We had Evelyn Laye, Yehudi Menuhin, lots of famous names, and we had dances every Saturday night They were "excuse me" dances all the time, as you can imagine, given the number of girls there.

But in some ways it was a very sad posting, because we'd look out one day and see the Flow absolutely full of destroyers, and the next morning they'd be gone, on the Russian convoys, although we didn't know that at the time. Half of them didn't come back.

Rita Marsden, - Childwall

Lights Out

I joined because I thought it would be exciting to do something different... I was only seventeen and a half.

The first night, we got ready for bed, curlers in and all that, and we'd been told about the various bells for different things thoughout the day, and she told us to make sure we got down to the regulating office early in the morning, when you heard the bell. So this girl and me, we were tired out, travelling, we went to bed early. Put all our rollers in, washed and so on...and went to sleep.

I heard the bell, took the rollers out, make up on, dressed, walking down the corridor. An officer stopped us and asking us where we thought we were going ."On duty, ma'am"

She said "Get back to bed, that's the 'lights out' bell".

I think the uniform was attractive, because when we went to dances, in Chatham, the girls in civilian clothes used to say "oh, here's the WRENS" coming in we won't get a dance now."

Eileen O'Connor-Knotty Ash

And mother came, too

My mother came with me of course, because in those days - it was 1942, you didn't go on your own, and when I saw the poster for the WRNS, I decided there and then.

We were sent to the Blundellsands Hotel, it was beautiful, and Walkers used to supply all the drink, and us Wrens used to run down to talk to the drivers. We had quite a few dates from that!

worked in the shop, and other days, you'd go on the minesweepers. They were originally fishing smacks, and the engines were a bit like car engines. We'd always be covered in grease, but I loved it.

Nearly all the men we worked with were Chief Petty Officers, they'd been motor mechanics in civilian life. They

Left : Winifred Green, 1942.
Above: *MMS 1019*, Winifred Green on board during sea trials.

Most of the girls wanted to be stewards, and I thought "I've had enough of that at home" - your mother had you doing everything then. So I was put in the sewing room, where they used to alter the uniforms to fit. I stayed there for six months, I had the "life of Riley".

We wore the sailors blue and white tops, and bellbottoms.

My next posting was to Morpeth Dock, the minesweeper base, and I went on the engines. Some days you

looked after us, most of them were married, and they were like brothers to us, no hanky panky or anything like that. I mean, we all fancied them but we did nothing about it.

Further along the quayside another six Wrens repaired the sweep when it was damaged, and we had two girls who went aboard each ship cleaning the Lewis guns.

We all used to go for gun practice along the Overhead railway to HMS "*Eaglet*".

We lived in a large house in Prenton which had been converted for us, they took all the carpets out as well as the lovely bed and they filled it with iron bunks, four to each room.

When the overhaul was finished on a minesweeper, they'd take us out to the bar, and we used to fish out there, and net lovely plaice and that.

Winifred Green-Tuebrook

WRNS, CIPOs and POs outside engineers workshops, Morpeth Dock, 1943.

Waving the Flag

My dad was in the navy and he'd been killed in the war, he was on a merchant cruiser, the HMS "*Jarvis Bay*". I was 16 then, so I joined the WRNS when I was 18.

There was a naval base at Alsager, and I worked in the Chief's mess there, waiting on. I was transferred then to Skegness, a training base for sailors lcarning wireless and so on. You used to hear the music, and they'd be waving their flags in time to the rhythm, learning semaphore.

Lily Leyland-Knotty Ash

Allotments

I remember going with my mother, to the different shipping offices. I used to love going to Harrisons, they had all the names of the ships on the wall there.

The various shipping companies headquarters used to be oak panelled, full of leather seats, elaborate to what we were used to. My mother would have a yellow form, the cashier would take it and give her the "allotment".

Theresa Bassett-Aigburth

A silver spoon

I started at Elder Dempster in November 1947, it was like being part of a big family. There were some cargo vessels that carried 12 passengers, mostly coast staff and missionaries travelling to and from Africa, and if a ship had a cargo for the Continent, it would call at Dover to land the passengers, and 12 office staff would then be

WREN Lily Leyland (back row right) and friends.
Below: Blue Funnel Menu cover
Leadbetter's Cockatoo - Australia.

allowed to do the coastal trip, for the mere cost of 7/6d a day.

I did that trip on the "*Shonga*", heading for Copenhagen and Aarhus, and when we arrived, the second engineer asked me if I'd like to go to the Tivoli Gardens with him. He bought me a silver sugar spoon, which is still in use today!

We were married in 1956. Elders did not allow children on board, but when they joined with Blue Funnel, we were able to take our daughters, and they were the first of Elders sea staff to go.

Audrey Stubbs-Warrington

Ship's husband

I joined Cunard, in the cash deparment in 1952, and in the end I finished up as Fleet, Personnel and Welfare officer. The job was actually "ship's husband" which is a funny name for a woman, but if anyone was sick or in trouble, I had to go and sort it out...24 hours a day. We were very proud of Cunard, we used to say we were the lowest paid shipping clerks in the country but we were paid in tradition.

Leadbeater's Cockatoo   Australia

THE BLUE FUNNEL LINE

I also worked for the company doctor, the crew had to be perfectly fit, and I used to say the most difficult job in the world was to get a Chinese crewman ..who had no English.. to give a sample of urine.

The laundries were mine, I had to staff them. People don't think about laundries but they have all the bedding to do, the soft furnishings, all the fancy items from First Class, and all course all the white suits when they go out to the tropics, they have to be starched. When they were hanging up on the line, they looked like headless men.

In the Falklands War, you know, all my girls - all from Liverpool, volunteered to go on the QEII.

Their mothers minded their babies and children, and they all came back, with a Falklands medal. I was very proud of them.

Jenny Kemp-Waterloo

Change your water

When we came into port, we came into the west wall of Gladstone dock, and the women who used to come aboard were various ages, some were pushing 60.

Now, all the hot water came from a huge cauldron on the dock, and the women were set up in gangs, one on port and one on starboard.

There was a big lady in charge, I can see her still, with a big bun on the back of her head. These ladies would go down and wash all the paintwork in the cabins, so in order to change the water in their buckets, this charge hand lady used to shout down the gangway "Change your water, girls"

The port side women would come down the steep gangway, top their buckets up and go back, and then the starboard women would be called to

Queen Elizabeth II in the Mersey.

96

change their water.

Now we had a bloke on board who was a brilliant mimic, Rooney his name was, and while the charge hand was shouting to one gang of women, he was shouting to the other...

So they all came up at once bumping into one another, and you could hear all terrible arguing going on.

Bruce Ferguson-Runcorn

Keep it Clean

When my mother got ready of a morning, the bucket came first. She had all her equipment in the bucket, scrubbing brush, floor cloth, she used to wrap the cloth around the bucket, put a bar of soap in, tuck the cloth round the handle and I'd see her, trotting up the road, with this bucket over her arm.

They wore flowered pinnies in those days, with big pockets, she never wore a turban, but she wore a net to keep her hair out of her eyes.

They had a lady who got them all together, they called her the "blocker", she knew where they drank in the local pubs, because obviously they had no phones then...she was called Lizzie Donnelly.

Sometimes my mum would collect neighbours, you know, ask them if wanted to go,and some would do it for the money, they'd get their buckets, too.

They all drank in the same pubs, when the job was finished...at the pubs in town, or some of them lived in Old Swan, they'd go in the Cygnet there. They used to stand at the bar, in a group. Probably all the wages would go, but I don't know what they did with the buckets!

It was very very hard work, when she came home she was really tired. They had to scrub decks, their knees would be sore.

She'd get down to town and travel by the Overhead Railway to the various docks, sometimes the job would only last a few days, but other times, she'd go from one ship to another. She used to talk about the various vessels, the "*Mauretania*" or the "*Reina Del*", as she called it.

Sometimes she'd come home with flour bags, and she'd make sheets out of them. But some of them used to wrap the real things under their clothes, towels and everything, and one got caught once. There was a policeman on the gates, and he must have picked at random, and of course, this woman looked enormous because she had all this bedding and stuff wrapped round her. I remember my mother was real worried about it. You've got to remember that things were very hard in those days, the money was a pittance for the work they did, and clothing was on ration. I can remember my mother getting sent home one day, she had a nose bleed, with the kneeling down and scrubbing, she had high blood pressure but in those days, they just carried on, you know, with life. And she would lose her money for that.

A lot of the women were in their 60's.

She took my sister once, and she was only young. She was out of work at the time, she used to work on the milk, pulling the carts around at one time, so she went with my mum.

Sue Iddon-Speke

Butter wouldn't melt

I remember the catering strike, we had the "*Britannic*" and the "*Ascania*" full of passengers ready to sail, and they all walked off. This was at the end of of the 50s, John Prescott, now the deputy prime minister, was involved in it. The office staff volunteered to go down.
Oh, the mess! We were down in the galley trying to cook the food, and we were walking on squashed peas and all sorts.
I was given the butter patter, a great big machine with little silver dishes and you had to put a dish under the spout, pull the handle and little pats of butter would come out.
What I didn't know was that they'd put this great block of butter in the machine in the morning and it had melted. I pulled this handle and a stream of melted butter shot all over me. I had to be sent home in a taxi to change.
We were on nearly a week 'til they went back…and at the end of it all, we were shattered, and when we got back to work.. all we got was a pound note for all we'd done.

Jenny Kemp-Waterloo

A lovely job

I was working in a hairdressers in Allerton Road, and I applied, through George Henry Lees, for a job at sea. I thought it'd be an adventure.
I sailed on the "*Apapa*" to West Africa. This would be 1956. There were five women on board, the nanny, three stewardesses, and me.
We answered to the Chief Steward, and his word was law.
I worked in a shop, more or less one room, it stocked everything, and the barbers was one side, the ladies hairdressers on the other.
It was a lovely job, my day started at nine o'clock because you had to fit in with mealtimes. I finished at 12, didn't work in the afternoon, I'd sit on deck and read and relax, then work from four 'til seven.
When we went into a port, the Customs would come on board and seal the shop, so I was free to do as I liked. It was the 'Life of Riley', I loved it.
We were chaperoned everywhere…
I remember arriving in Bathurst, and some of the local men had five or six wives behind them, all dressed the same, so you knew which man they belonged to.

Jean Gallagher-Gateacre

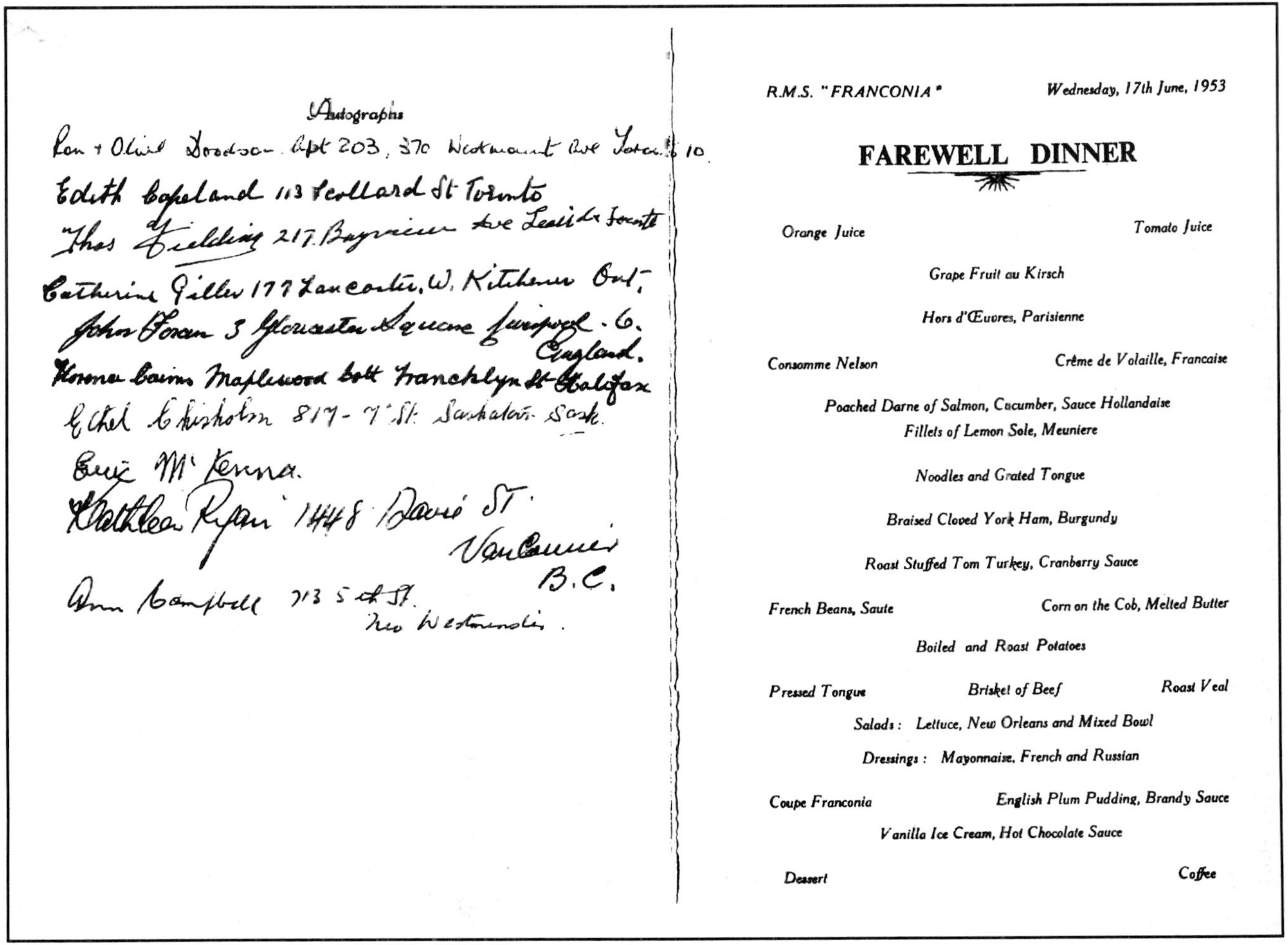

Autographs

Ron + Olive Dodson Apt 203, 370 Westmount Ave Toronto 10.

Edith Copeland 113 Scollard St Toronto

Thos Fielding 217 Bayview Ave Leaside Toronto

Catherine Giller 177 Lancaster W. Kitchener Ont.

John Foran 3 Gloucester Square Liverpool 6. England.

Florence Cairns Maplewood Cott Franchlyn St Halifax

Ethel Chisholm 817 - 7th St. Saskatoon Sask.

Eric McKenna.

Kathleen Ryan 1448 Davie St. Vancouver B.C.

Ann Campbell 713 5th St. New Westminster.

R.M.S. "FRANCONIA" Wednesday, 17th June, 1953

FAREWELL DINNER

Orange Juice Tomato Juice

Grape Fruit au Kirsch

Hors d'Œuvres, Parisienne

Consomme Nelson Crême de Volaille, Francaise

Poached Darne of Salmon, Cucumber, Sauce Hollandaise
Fillets of Lemon Sole, Meuniere

Noodles and Grated Tongue

Braised Cloved York Ham, Burgundy

Roast Stuffed Tom Turkey, Cranberry Sauce

French Beans, Saute Corn on the Cob, Melted Butter

Boiled and Roast Potatoes

Pressed Tongue Brisket of Beef Roast Veal

Salads: Lettuce, New Orleans and Mixed Bowl

Dressings: Mayonnaise, French and Russian

Coupe Franconia English Plum Pudding, Brandy Sauce

Vanilla Ice Cream, Hot Chocolate Sauce

Dessert Coffee

RMS '*Franconia*' - Farewell Dinner Menu 17th June 1953... with autographs.

Keeping them in check

Years ago, whoever took on the stewardesses for Cunard, on sailing day, she'd come on board and they all used to wipe their lipstick off, they'd have the grey stockings on and flat heels.'
Of course, as soon as the ship sailed, they'd be all downstairs, putting their "lippy" back on and changing into nylons, and high heels. And instead of putting their hat on the front, they'd tip it on the back of their heads.

Norman Broadbent-Childwall

Message in a Bottle

I retired when I was sixty, and I got a beautiful mink jacket. But at the end of the first week, they wanted people for the plate house on the *QE11* and there was no one to recruit them, so they asked me to go back.
I got another ten years out of them, and I was the oldest shipping clerk in the country.
I had a ship in a bottle this time for my leaving present, but it isn't even a Cunard vessel!

Jenny Kemp-Waterloo

Chapter Seven: The'pool

It's Canning Place for me today
Maybe I'll get a ship at the 'pool
To far flung foreign ports of call
When next I leave Liverpool

Ask people what's changed the most in their city, and they'll say the river and the docks. They mourn the loss of the Overhead Railway and the hustle and bustle of what was once 'The Gateway to the World.'

The Merchant Navy Memorial, Pier Head, Liverpool.

Cobbles and cart horses

In 1930, I was an office boy, making long journeys on foot along the dock road, delivering letters. There was a deafening noise of iron shod cart wheels and the tramp of shire horses on the cobbles. A forest of ship's funnels and clouds of black smoke. The screeching of chains and crane pulleys. There was a smell of coal mingled with the cooking from dockside cocoa rooms. I remember, after much tramping and delivering, collapsing on a chair in one of the cafes, with a mug of hot tea and a "wet nellie" - a penny in old money.

Jim Rehill-Allerton

Bird's eye view

In the thirties, it was exciting to look down from John Holt's office in the Liver Building onto the Overhead Railway and see the streams of traffic, including cart horses pulling heavy loads. One of our windows gave us a grandstand view past the pier at New Brighton, and at high tide, cruise liners and merchants ships were piloted backwards and forwards, you could see them on both sides of the Mersey.

Bettina Thomson-Spital

The port stood still

I met a friend who'd just become a telegram boy, so I joined too. My "beat", for delivering, was from Huskisson North to Gladstone Dock, and all the southern ports were closed, so all the big passenger ships, bringing troops and so on, had to come to Liverpool, so I saw ships that never ever came here - the beautiful Castle Line ships, the Orient Line, P & O, many companies which have now disappeared.

In fact, I was on the dock one day when one of the Princess Line ships, came in and he blew the whistle as he passed Perch Rock. That noise stopped the docks for ten minutes

Harry Hignett-Wallasey

Fairyland

On the ground floor of the Cunard building (which used to be open right at the front, to the Pier Head, before Brocklebanks blocked it off), during the early summer when the sun was setting, all the marble went pink, it was like a fairy land.

Captain Price had his place on the roof, he was the hydrographer, he charted the tides for all over the world ..and he had this little house up there, with thousands and thousands of charts all rolled up in little pidgeon holes, it was magic.

The experimental chef was always in the Cunard Building, he would try out dishes, he brought down frogs legs for me to try. We also had four seamstresses, they used to do the darning, I mean you didn't throw a sheet away with a little hole in it, they'd go backwards and forwards with

"Stormcock", working in the Cammell Laird wet basin, 1963- reproduced by permission of Reflections c/o www.20thcenturyimages.com

lovely thick cotton thread to cover the hole...the decorative architects were on the sixth floor...one of their big jobs was the main square of all Cunard ships had linolcum in a beautiful pattern, and they used to paint the patterns up there.

In Marsh Lane, they did all the repairs to the fine woodwork on board. I had to go down every week to the bottling stores, with 1/6d for fish for the cats, they were there to catch the rats, and they were like tigers!

Jenny Kemp-Waterloo

A vision

I can remember looking down into the Gladstone Graving Dock when the the brand new *"Mauretania"*, which was then the largest passenger ship to be built in England, had been brought over from Lairds. The dock yard workers were playing football underneath the ship...that vision stuck in my mind.

Alan McLelland-Mossley Hill

Dredging

I joined the Dock Board in the marine department, dredgers and other work, taking all the sand out of the docks. You'd fill buckets, scoop out the silt, and drop it into the hopper, then out to the bar to drop it.

During the war there were magnetic

mines dropped by the Luftwaafe, and there was a lot of lives lost through ships blowing up in the river. We used to see Bootle and Liverpool ablaze when we were out, we'd be away a week, and I was always anxious about my family. It was worse than being at war. We got the Atlantic Star for sailing through dangerous waters - the Mersey.

William Tennant-Bootle

and Fred, the other apprentice, and myself were sent to the "*Heemskerk*". On our first morning, the dock was quiet, so we took a chance and slipped off to the Liverpool City Caterers canteen, which was just outside the main dock gates. It was just before noon, and we were very pleased with ourselves, thinking we would have our dinner before our mates.

But we were brought down to earth

The early bird...

I served my apprenticeship in the Repair Engine Department in Cammell Laird. In August 1943, and after 16 months, I was sent over to Gladstone Dock...we were taken over by a fleet of Wallasey Corporation buses.

The battleship HMS "*Duke of York*" and the Dutch cruiser "*Jacob van Heemskerk*" were in dry dock there

Blue Funnel *"Calchas"* entering Alfred Dock, circa 1959. Reproduction by permission of marine artist Les Cowle.
Overleaf: Landing stage, the Waterfront Buildings and Canning half tide basin.

with a bang when the girl behind the counter told us that all the dinners had gone, and if we wanted anything in future, we'd have to be up earlier in the day. We soon got into the run of things, and at 11.30 we used to walk up to the British Restaurant in Seaforth.

In a way it was a catch-22 situation - when you were working at Gladstone, you were told to behave yourself, or find yourself back at the yard - and over at Lairds, they told you the opposite.

The offices Lairds were using at that time were formerly used by the Royal Navy during the war, and underneath the paint on the door of the office you could see the words "Intelligence Room". I was proud to work there, and I believe that during the "golden years" they built an average of one vessel for every 20 days, and at the same time the repair yard worked on 120 warships, as well as repairs to over 2000 merchant vessels.

Dave Thompson-Irby

Nearly all out

The port was full of ship's engineers and repairers then, there was Harland and Wolff, Mulhearns, Browns, Evans, Russells and many more.

One job in those days was the cargo gear had to be taken off and tested, boilers to be cleaned and repaired. Any machine work was always done by the ship repairing crew, and the work in the engine room was done by shore men, too. Nowadays, it's done by ship's engineers.

When I started ships were being converted from coal burners to oil, the gang was normally a chargehand, an appentice and three or four fitters.

One day there was a call - "Right lads, everybody out" - so the chargehand gave me the repair list, because apprentices weren't ever allowed to

strike. So all the men went off, from Gladstone Dock, got the Overhead to Huskisson and walked up to Crichtons. When they got there, there was no strike at all. It was a docker, he did it for a joke.

David Eccles-Aigburth

Weavils in the bread

I was on two strikes, the first one Billy Hart got six month in gaol, it was over conditions and money, around 1948/9. Some ships had terrible conditions, atrocious food. Weavils...well, we used to "x ray" the bread (hold it up to the light), and it'd be full of them. We'd take the middle out and just eat the crust. That was regular. Some firms were worse than others.

So, we walked off and then the lads wouldn't sign, so all the ships were held up.

Billy Hart used to stand outside in the square by the Pool in Paradise Street. He was arrested. They said *we* couldn't go on strike because we were the King's Merchant Navy, and we were breaking our contract...so we all had to go back.

Bill Sheridan-Netherton

In your lunch hour

I got a job as a junior clerk on the general manager's staff of the then Mersey Docks and Harbour Board. On the traffic and warehouse committee, making sure goods flowed across the quays...this was 1954.

I'd always walked the dock estate as a teenager, of course the port was still

Liverpool Pierhead, 1949

then the second port of the U.K. My boss was of the tough old school. I remember he said I ought to familiarise myself with the estate, so I said "When should I go", and he replied "You have a lunch hour".

So in my lunch hour, I discovered this tiny ship in the south end discharging a cargo of fruit, from Spain, which they'd distributed all over the floor of the shed, and were selling off the quay, which was forbidden. Liverpool Quays then were so busy that there were bye laws which said everything had to be moved as soon as possible. So they would have been promptly charged a quay rent for that. This wasn't a regular incident, though.

I remember that it became known that some clandestine activity might be going on in a shed where Guinness was brought in, and it was thought people were staying behind to play pitch and toss, so I was told to go down (again, in my lunch hour).

I walked up to the gate, at Salthouse Dock, and suddenly a great fist came through the doorway and grabbed me by the throat, and shook me, and said "What do you want", and I struggled for breath. He looked at my suit, as I told him I was from the Dock Board, and he said, brushing me down, "Why didn't you say so?"

In the meantime, all the sounds of chinking and so on had ceased. We never did discover if anything had been going on.

Alan McLelland-Mossley Hill

Traditions

When I left school I went to work in Cammell Lairds. My two grandfathers, my dad and his six brothers, and uncles on my mother's side, all worked there, so it was a tradition. There were no ifs and buts, my father told me I was going in the shipyard. I started in the costing department, I was too young at 15 to start an apprenticeship. One of my jobs was to pick up all the foreman's overtime slips.

They built the *"Fighting Cock"* and *"Game Cock"* tugs, at the same time as the *"Ark Royal"* and it was reputed that the apprentices built the tugs with the metal from the *"Ark Royal"*, but I don't know if that was true. I think that was 1953. I lived outside Cammell Lairds, in Tranmere, and I used to watch the men going to work, and I think there were about 18,000 men there at the peak, just after the war.

There were seven slipways, and ships were being built at a fantastic rate. Especially on a summer's day, you could hear the riveters' hammers, the noise was amazing, bangs, booms, a hive of activity.

You could see the ships from when they first laid the keel until the day of the launch, and you could stand at the top of the hill and watch ships being launched. They'd go down the slipway, and then the tugs would race after them, they only had half an hour to pick up the ship, she had no engines or assistance other than the tugs.

Alan Richards-Ledsham

107

Looking through the glass

I remember the "*Windsor Castle*" being launched at Cammell Lairds, and the old captain of the tug I was on came out with a telescope so I could look at her...we were on the other side of the river.

Owen Lawler-Maghull

Famous Funnels

All Elders ships were well known, we had the famous buff funnel, and across the docks from us you used to have the Harrison Lines, which was two of fat and one of lean, two white rings and a red ring in the middle on their funnels.

Ronald Vaughan-West Derby

A big job - painting the funnel of Harrison vessel *"Settler"*

Industrial Music

I went to work as a messenger boy for the engineers department in Gladstone Dock. I knew every inch of the port, all the shipping companies, repairers like Harland and Wolff, carters, ships' victuallers.

The smells of the port were molasses, peanuts, rubber, teak, spices. The sounds were like industrial music - you had the horses, the bogies working the ships, the winches, people always shouting - a cacophony of wonderful things to hear.

I was there when they had a big fire at Gladstone Dock, a rubber fire, and the whole shed burned down with about 30,000 tons of rubber. The whole thing melted, and the graving dock north to Alex, was paved with a foot and a half of rubber. The Mersey Docks decided to remove this, and it looked like they were flensing whales, they had fellows with forks, lifting it, and others cutting it...that'd be about 1948/9.

The whole of the port was a dangerous place to be. Cargoes were dangerous then, for instance, you had hide and anthrax was a big worry.

Stan Amos-Moreton

All sorts

The port then was mad busy, ships everywhere, loading and unloading, for weeks, they were not in and out like they are now.

That's when the trouble started. Men would knock nails through their feet, fall down ladders, come back drunk end up in in the dock. I'd have to them up to hospital to have t... stomach pumped, because the stuff in the docks was appalling then. And of course they used to unload from the holds, with cranes, in those days, no containers, and if they were bringing anything in that they thought we'd like, they used to drop one, they'd drop a case of liquorice allsorts, and it would come up to the office in a big solid block. We used to cut it up and weigh it on the letter scales, so we all got the same.

Jenny Kemp-Waterloo

Going down the 'pool

Back in 1943, I received my calling up papers, to be a Bevan Boy, going down the mines, but my Auntie Beatie had a good friend who was in the Merchant Navy, he was a bosun, and he offered to take me down to the Shipping Federation, the Pool, to see if I could get a job.
The Pool was just further on from where the Moat House is now, in Paradise Street. What you did, you went to the Federation and handed your card in, they used to have a big blackboard up, and what ships were going that day and what crew they required.
If you saw a ship you fancied, you'd go to the counter and ask, they'd give you a chit, you'd take it down to the ship, in Canada, or Huskisson or Herculaneum this side, or perhaps the Blue Funnel boats in Wallasey, and make yourself known to the second steward. He'd ask to see your discharge book, to see what kind of discharge you'd had from your last ship. "G" was for good, "VG" was very good, but if you had a "VNC" in your book, that meant "Voyage Not Completed", you'd jumped ship somewhere.

Norman Broadbent-Childwall

Empress of Scotland", Pier Head, with Bruce Ferguson

Bugle Boys

I was a recruitment officer for P&O. They had a large fleet of fast refrigerated ships sailing as the Federal Line, from Sandon or Gladstone Docks to Australia and New Zealand, full to the brim with manufactured goods and returning six weeks later with dairy products and meat.

One of my ancilliary duties was to audition Deck Boy Buglers - 16 year olds who had just finished their sea training at the "*Indefatigable*". The auditions took take the lads through various bugle calls used on cadet ships, the two I remember were the "*Rakaia*" and "*Otaio*".

I often wonder what the businessmen and women must have thought, in Water Street below, hearing "reveille" coming from the roof of the office building!

Alex Cross-Wallasey

Romance of the river

In those days, all over Merseyside, Everton Valley, Birkenhead, New Brighton, you could hear all the tugs working, in the middle of the night some people would be woken up by the whistles. It was romantic I suppose.

The port was that busy then, they used to have three big dredgers, they'd work constantly, 24 hours a day, to keep the port open. Now, the entrances to the likes of the Brunswick dock are silted up, many are blocked off, and it's all new housing and offices.

There used to be pubs we'd go to, the "Seven Steps", The "Blazing Stump" in Birkenhead, the "Carradoc" and of course, the "Bramley Moore".

Alan Richards-Ledsham

Say it with flowers

Liverpool was great, it was a real port then. The pubs along the dock road were legendary, full of seamen and dockers.

I remember going out with a pal and I was late, so I bought some flowers for my wife. I was self conscious going in these pubs, and a huge docker came up to me and said "Don't worry, mate, I'm in the same boat" - and produced another bunch from underneath his coat.

Brian McEvoy-Wallasey

Good times ashore

My memories of the port are fond, We'd go to the "big house" on the corner and then to the Crown in Lime Street, that was well used by seamen and then we'd go down to the Merchant Navy club, the top end of Church Street.

Then when the pubs closed, everyone would go up to the Grafton or the Rialto. We'd all have our American suits on, you know. They use to call us Cunard Yanks in those days. To show that you were a "Cunard Yank", you'd put a packet of "Lucky Strikes" on counter and always leave the change on the counter, like the Americans used to...it was just showing off, really.

Norman Broadbent-Childwall

"Antenor" and tugs, in the Mersey. Reproduction by permission of marine artiest Les Cowle

Whisky and milk

I was living then in the sailors' home. You had a little six foot by eight foot cubicle, had your meals there. It was in Paradise Street, where the hotel is now. In Paradise Street there was a little place for boy seamen, a Mrs. Woods used to look after us there.

We used to drink in Ma Shepherds, corner of Cases Street, she always sat in the corner with whisky and milk.

I used to leave my allotment in the post office then, you could only draw £3 a day, so I used to go to the pool, and if there were no jobs, I'd take my book to Ma Shepherd, she'd give me £3, the next day I'd go to the post office, go to Ma's, and get my book back, she never charged extra.

Arthur Burch-Woolton

Wave warning

We used to drink in O'Connors in Lime Street, and once the pubs closed at 10 o'clock, everyone went to the Marionette Club, in Lime Street - all the sailors went there.

You used to have the good time girls around there, but we were warned by an officer about what not to do.

If the girls waved at you, you were supposed to just wave back.

Harry Day-Old Roan

All for show

We used to come into Liverpool on a Tuesday. There was a guy from Milner Raynors, and he used to sell us uniforms You were paying so much every trip ...every docking day he'd be there with his little book, collecting.

If you couldn't afford the nice shirts, he would sell us cardboard cuffs and cardboard fronts and cardboard collars. I'd get a pack of twelve of each, and all you needed underneath was a vest.

So you'd have your immaculate dinner jacket on with everything else cardboard. They were brilliant.

Roy Chambers-Llandudno

All front

We only had two white shirts, so we bought "dickie fronts", a little piece of white cotton with four pieces of string, which you tied around your back.

Harry Day-Old Roan

The gear

When I went away to sea, Wilkie took me down to a little outfitters in Garston, by the docks, got me rigged out - at nine at night.

Arthur Burch-Woolton

A bob a night

We used to stay at the Gordon Smith Institute, on the corner of Duke Street. You got a room with a bunk in, I think we paid about a shilling a night.

Roy Chambers-Llandudno

The way we were in 1956. *Cheshire*, just launched from Cammell Lairds', is guided from the river by the busy tugs into the fitting out basin at the shipyard.

The One O'clock Gun

The one o'clock gun was operated by the landing stage seaman at Woodside cattle stage. The gun was from the 1914 war.

I used to leave the stage master's hut at half past twelve, go to the gun, at Morpeth. You'd have to open the magazine, and the gun housing. You then got your percussion cap and charge. You'd check everything, and have a test fire at five to one, just with a stick to trigger the mechanism.

You had a clock there, it was a hundred years old but still spot on, and if that gun didn't fire when it got to one o'clock, you stuck your stick in to fire it, Invariably, we had to fire it because it was operated by a telephone line which was nearly always broken.

Having done that, you had to clean the gun with soda and water, pull through, you then greased it, locked up and made everything secure...It took an hour for that one second blast.

Stan Amos-Moreton

The One O'clock Gun - Birkenhead.

Courtesy Ian Bouma

Another time, another place

We used to travel to Gladstone Dock as apprentices, on the old Overhead Railway...In those days, there wasn't room for a rowing boat - Harrison, Elders, Cunard, Clan Line - oh, so many....
Now I'm so sad, why can't I show my sons what I loved?

Colin Sharp-Bromborough

The end of an Era - Demolition of the Overhead Railway

LIFE AT LAIRDS - Memories of working shipyard men
by David Roberts

When Cammell Lairds has gone and we are a generation or two down the line who will answer the questions 'What did they do there?' 'What was it like?' This book answers the questions. - Sea Breezes

A Piece of Social History – Liverpool Echo

Life at Lairds is a book of more than 120 pages about what life was like for the thousands of ordinary people that worked in the world famous Birkenhead shipyard. Contains many rare photographs of Lairds, its' ships and its' surroundings.

ISBN 0 9521020 1 3 £6.99 + £1.50 p&p

Faster Than the Wind - A History Guide to the Liverpool to Holyhead Telegraph.
by Frank Large

Take a journey along the one of most spectacular coastlines in Britain, the beautiful hills and countryside of North Wales and Wirral. On a clear day it is possible to see just how signals were sent along the coast to and from Liverpool. This book contains full details of the intriguing and little known sites of the substantial remains of the Liverpool to Holyhead Telegraph Stations. A second journey can then be taken into the fascinating workings of such a telegraph and those people involved in creating and using the signalling system and what life was really like living and working at the telegraph stations more than 100 years ago.

ISBN 09521020 9 9   £8.95 + £1.50 p&p

Iron Clipper – 'Tayleur' – the White Star Line's 'First Titanic'
by H.F. Starkey

'Iron Clipper' is subtitled 'The First Titanic' for it tells the story of the first White Star liner to be lost on her maiden voyage. Built on the Upper Mersey at Warrington, the *'Tayleur'* tragedy of 1854 and the *'Titanic'* catastrophe of 1912 are disasters which have so much in common that the many coincidences make this factual book appear to be a work which is stranger than fiction.

ISBN 1 902964 00 4   £7.50+ £1.40 p&p

Schooner Port - Two Centuries of Upper Mersey Sail
by H.F. Starkey

Schooner Port tells the story of the part Runcorn and navigation of the upper Mersey played in the Industrial Revolution and of the contribution of merchants, the shipbuilders, and the crews in making Britain 'The Workshop of the World'. Also recounted is something of the courage and tragedy, which was the lot of many flatmen and seamen who helped build British industry on the strength of the shipping fleet.

'Recognised as the only authoritative work on this particular subject ' - Sea Breezes

'Packed with hard facts and illustrated with some rare old photographs, this rare book should command a wide readership'. - Liverpool Echo

ISBN 0 9521020 5 6   £8.95 + £1.50 p&p

THE GOLDEN WRECK - THE TRAGEDY OF THE ROYAL CHARTER
by ALEXANDER MCKEE

The effects great of the great hurricane of October 1859 were to shock the nation. 133 ships were sunk, 90 were badly damaged and almost 800 people lost their lives. More than half of those that perished were on one ship - The *Royal Charter*.

The Royal Charter has a special place in maritime history as one of the greatest ever peacetime disasters. Her story too is one of incredible bad luck...had she come to grief just yards away from the unforgiving rocks that destroyed her she would have grounded upon a stony beach where it is likely that most of her passengers and crew would have been able to walk off.

She was also an extraordinary vessel in that she belonged to that crossover period between sail and steam when the steam engine was unproven and unreliable, not only that but coal was bulky and expensive whilst the wind, though erratic, was free of charge. She was a compromise, a sailing ship with an engine, not a main engine but a small 'auxiliary' engine that would be used when the wind eluded her, to power the vessel to try and 'find the wind'. Furthermore the Royal Charter moved away from the tried and tested design of the fast clippers that were constructed of wood... she was made of iron.

She was built at Sandycroft on the River Dee, the next-door neighbour to the river that was to become her home...the River Mersey. Soon after she was launched...sideways because of her great size for the day, she perhaps seemed ill starred in that whilst being towed down the river she grounded upon a sandbank off Flint, North Wales, and suffered serious damage to her main keel.

On her maiden voyage to Australia she had to turn back to Plymouth, England after discovering that she did not respond correctly to her steering and shipping too much water during a moderate gale... she was in Plymouth for 20 days. She eventually completed her maiden voyage to Melbourne in record time and her owners were able to boast about their new service 'England to Australia in under 60 days'.

Just a few short years later she was returning home and was hours away from disembarking her charges in Liverpool... until, when rounding Anglesey on the northern coast of Wales...disaster struck in the form of a Force 12 hurricane.

The people of the small village of Moelfre, Anglesey came to the aid of the vessel and those from the ship who tried to escape the lashing waves and the deadly rocks. News of the wreck soon spread and the *Royal Charter's* other cargo, gold, became the focus of people's attention. Was all of it ever recovered? If not where did it go? The *Royal Charter's* gold still has the power to attract the adventurous and this book also explores attempts at salvage and treasure hunting more than 140 years on. £9.50 & 1.50 p&p ISBN 1 902964020

JUST NUISANCE AB - His full story
by Terence Sisson

The amazing but true story of the only dog that was officially enlisted into British Royal Navy, a Great Dane whose name was Nuisance, his official rank and name was AB Just Nuisance. Famed for his preference for the company of navy ratings (he wasn't too keen on Officers) in and around the famous World War II naval base of Simonstown, South Africa, Nuisance helped many a sailor rejoin his ship after a night on the town. Today his own statue overlooking the bay off the Cape of Good Hope commemorates AB Just Nuisance. £7.50 & £1.20 p&p

A Welcome in the Hillsides?
- The Merseyside & North Wales Experience of Evacuation 1939-1945
by Jill Wallis

A book that is both informative and moving, with the stories of the thousands of children who left the dangers of Merseyside for the safety of North Wales during World War II.
ISBN 1 9029640 13 6   £9.95 + £1.60 p&p

VIDEOS
Cammell Laird - Old Ships and Hardships - the story of a shipyard.

After an extensive search for moving footage of this world famous shipyard at work a video of the history of this shipyard has at last been compiled. How Cammell Laird served the nation through two World Wars, building world famous vessels like the *Rodney, Hood, Mauritania, Ark Royal, Windsor Castle* and many more, up to the tragic day in 1993 when Lairds was shut down.

The story of the yard is also told through the voices of the men who worked at Lairds; Welders, cranedrivers, electricians and plumbers, they tell of the hardships of building ships in all weathers and the lighter moments that came from some of the 'characters' of the yard.

£14.99 including post and packaging in UK.

'All in a Day's work.' Volumes I & II
– a look at working lives on the River Mersey.

Just when you might have thought that the River Mersey was dead and buried the biggest surprise of all comes along. There is life in the old dog yet! The River Mersey is alive and well. Liverpool, Birkenhead, Tranmere, Eastham and Runcorn are still places that enjoy marine traffic and employ people working on the river. There are interviews with River Pilots, shipbuilders, shiprepairers, tugmen and dredgermen that show that the age-old crafts and seamanship itself are still as strong as they ever were. There is also archive footage of working life on the river.

Features Rock Boats, Mersey Ferries, the Bunker boats & crews on the Mersey, the Vess Tracking System for river traffic, new vessels on the river, lockmasters and much more.

£14.99 including post and packaging in UK.

All videos are available in international formats for £17.99 + P&P £3.50.

Please state country/ format required.

To Order Books or Videos Direct Contact:-
Avid Publications, Garth Boulevard, Hr. Bebington, Wirral,Merseyside UK
CH63 5LS. Tel / Fax 0151 645 2047
Look at the books and videos via the internet on
http://www.avidpublications.co.uk
E-mail info@AvidPublications.co.uk